5-29

VCF-B07

TEACHER as ACTOR

MORRIS U. BURNS and PORTER S. WOODS

KENDALL/HUNT PUBLISHING COMPANY
2460 Kerper Boulevard   P.O. Box 539   Dubuque, Iowa 52004-0539

This edition has been printed directly from camera-ready copy.

Copyright © 1992 by Kendall/Hunt Publishing Company

ISBN 0-8403-7217-5

All rights reserved. No part of this publication may be reproduced,
stored in a retrieval system, or transmitted, in any form or by any
means, electronic, mechanical, photocopying, recording, or otherwise,
without the prior written permission of the copyright owner.

Printed in the United States of America
10 9 8 7 6 5 4 3 2 1

TABLE OF CONTENTS

CHAPTER 1
THE WORKSHOP

COMME ON DEVIENT GRAND MATHÉMATICIEN.

CHAPTER 1: THE WORKSHOP

I remember a conversation with a professor at our university as we crossed the campus to our offices after attending an early version of my workshop, the Teacher as Actor. He told me he was just a few months away from retirement, and the experience we had just shared had been exciting but also sad. He went on to explain that he had gone directly from undergraduate to graduate school, and then had begun teaching. He was now approaching forty years in the profession and never, in all this time, had he had a class or workshop on the art of teaching. Whatever else was going through his mind I don't know, but he thanked me again for the opportunity and expressed the hope that I would continue doing the workshop, particularly for people like him. His reaction and that of many others has led to the writing of this book.

For a number of years, I have taught theatre courses and directed plays on our campus. For the past decade I have also offered workshops for faculty on how to improve their teaching. What started as an idea for a service I could offer has gradually grown into what I believe is a practical and meaningful method. At no time did I think of the workshop as a "gimmick" or a way of selling a new approach. Quite frankly, at the outset I was not at all certain that it would be of any help to other teachers, particularly the diverse faculty we have on this campus, who teach everything from humanities to applied science. But through these sessions and other interactions with my colleagues, I have come to understand many of the strengths and possibilities of what might be called a methodology. This is what I want to share.

(Opposite) "How One Becomes a Mathematician," (Plate #3) lithograph,
Teachers and Students *by Honore Victorin Daumier.*

What led me to offer these sessions was my experience as a teacher. I teach acting almost every semester and deal with student actors in the plays I produce on campus. However, I also teach other types of classes. For example, I teach Theatre History in a lecture format and deal with advanced classes in a seminar format. In sharing my experiences with faculty in my program, I came to realize that we were all drawing on what we knew about acting in our varied roles as teachers. What began as a kind of bridge from one body of information to another, had grown into a useful means for improving our own classroom performances.

I began offering workshops for the faculty many years ago. From the beginning they were structured as though they were an acting class. I had a limit of twenty participants and used a mix of informal lecture demonstration and recitation. After trying a number of formats, I developed a day-long workshop.

Then and now I begin by describing the tools which teachers and actors share, proceed to exercises which are designed to energize a performer, and then deal with vocal production. After this warm-up, I describe "honesty" and then have the participants do exercises. This half of the workshop ends with lunch, during which we informally discuss points raised in the morning. When we reconvene, we describe "sub-text," those forms of indirect speech we all use when we communicate, and then do exercises based on this concept. We end the day with each class member giving a five minute lecture on a subject they choose. This is followed by a critiquing session in which I stress the points made during the day about effective communication. Usually the workshop ends with a request that they fill out evaluation forms and arrange visits to their classrooms, if they wish.

Each of these activities is represented by a chapter in the following text. My experiences in other people's classrooms, either first-hand or taken from writing or anecdote, are woven through the entire study. The other concerns discussed in these chapters are a brief study of acting as a discipline and the art of playwriting as a valuable aid to planning classes.

From the outset I felt that focussing the workshop's attention on both "acting" and "teaching" would be an interesting approach for faculty. I thought they would be intrigued to learn about acting and its connections with their own specialty. However, it turned out to be more than interesting and closer to serendipitous. I think this is because most faculty are extremely sensitive to what they perceive to be their weaknesses as teachers. On occasions too numerous to mention, veteran professors have told me about the lack of confidence they feel in front of a class, about the fear they have of any kind of peer review, and their nightmares about aggressive student evaluation systems. The approach I was taking seemed to calm some of their fears. In all honesty, we almost always lost a few participants when lunch came around after they have heard about the last exercise of the day: their chance to stand up and give a brief lecture. But most of them could defuse their anxiety during the day by responding to a new and interesting body of information. In trying to understand and apply what I was teaching them, they could stop worrying about peer evaluation of their presentational skills or their grasp of their field. For my part, I was careful to stress that I was not judging their competency and was only concerned about their understanding of the concepts I would be presenting during the day.

Following the same format used in the workshop, my text

begins with this introductory chapter, which outlines the approach used and the rationale behind it. I will then proceed to a discussion of acting, its theories, great teachers, and connection with our drama and culture. I next will describe exercises, useful to actors, which teachers can use to train their bodies and voices. Chapters on honesty and sub-text will follow, and then I will develop the concept of teacher as playwright. In this chapter, we will suggest ways of structuring lectures and seminars along lines suggested by theories of dramatic structure. There will be examples drawn from special lectures developed by teachers who deliberately explore the spaces between acting and teaching. The next chapter will be about teachers I have heard of or known and their particular approaches to the art. After this, I will attempt to tie it all together in a conclusion. My hope is that the text will parallel the experience of taking the workshop. What is missing is the "live" experience with the instructors and other workshop participants. This I can only approximate with anecdotes and examples, because teaching, after all, like acting, must be experienced directly to be truly effective.

The truth of this can be shown in what I believe to be a memorable example from the workshop. One class member was a young woman who was a biologist. She was quiet, self-assured, very attractive and though she had enjoyed what others were doing had seemed content to be audience. But when her turn came to give the five minute lecture, she explained that she often lectured on human sexuality. She then drew a graph on the blackboard at the front of the classroom. The vertical axis, she told us, was intensity and the horizontal was duration. Men, she reminded us, were much quicker to arrive at that level of excitement which she labelled as the "Big O." With her chalk she then drew a steep, quick mountain on the graph. By now we were all caught up in her explanation, but she was the picture of scientific objectivity. And then she explained that women were much slower in arriving at this level. Chalk in hand she began to draw a line which had a considerably slower angle of ascent than the average man's. Finally, she reached the upper corner of the board and then her line broke through the limits of the blackboard and she drew a high plateau across the wall. "And this state of excitement," she said," can go on and on and . . ." The class erupted in laughter. But maybe you had to be there.

TEACHING AND ACTING COMPARED

Some time ago I read about an actor who was hired by a famous law school to give lessons to the students on how to be effective in the courtroom. It turned out that the techniques being shared were tricks used to control or manipulate an audience and upstage anyone else. It was not what I wish to suggest when speaking of the connection between acting and related fields. Let me briefly describe this.

First, both the serious actor and the dedicated teacher are concerned with effective communication and committed to the information they are conveying. I can imagine many more permutations for effective teaching than for effective acting because the former is less constrained by matters of "style" and conventions than is acting. Actors may master the fundamentals of their craft in two or three years, but then they must learn how to do such theatre as Moliere's, Shakespeare's, and Neil Simon's for a variety of audiences and through several media, such as radio, television, and movies. This may seem like a lot, but remember there are as many ways to teach effectively as there are teachers.

Furthermore, it is important to note that a teacher could be said to be a playwright as well. After all, we must prepare our own material. Granted there have been actor-playwrights in our history, such as Moliere, Noel Coward, and Peter Ustinov, but they are exceptions to the rule. And how many actors are there who can expect an audience to return within a fortnight and take an examination on what they have retained from a performance?

I think most teachers would like to think of their profession in the terms used by Philip W. Jackson: "Teaching, characteristically, is a moral enterprise. The teacher, whether he admits it or not, is out to make the world a better place and its inhabitants better people."[1]

For the purposes of this study, I am considering neither the content of your lectures nor their match with your students' abilities. You know your field and can make accurate judgements about the appropriate levels for materials. I will, however, discuss the art of playwriting as a means for shaping a lecture and making it more interesting. Good teachers, like good actors, should understand the text they are presenting and be motivated to do it well. The differences among students are analogous to those that exist among different kinds of audiences. Shakespeare's tragedies may be very heavy going for young audiences; similarly, a lecture in physics assumes that the audience has the necessary background and maturity. Also, there are certain constraints placed on classroom presentations: the class time available, the number of meetings planned, and the need to achieve certain educational objectives. The end is effective teaching and clear communication, and not solely entertainment.

There is another remarkable difference between an actor and a teacher in terms of their relationships to a script. Actors may or may not like the characters they are portraying, but unless the issue is ultimately involved with the quality of the play, it is irrelevant. The actor's task is to make the character come alive on stage in accordance with the demands of the script regardless of how one might react to such a person in real life. It is often the case on stage that Judas is more interesting to play than Peter. The playwright is the god of this universe, and the trained actor fleshes out the character by careful study, understanding, imagination, and by finding those experiences in his or her own life which relate to the character's.

Teachers, on the other hand, have chosen the world in which they operate and are responsible for the scripts they develop. We hope you are teaching your preferred subject. The emotional and intellectual commitment to the material should be there. Your task is to share this enthusiasm and knowledge with your students and in the process avoid the sorts of confusion, frustration, and even anger which may result in "burn out." The teacher and the actor are both in danger of this when they forget why they are in front of the class or audience and begin to think of their "script" as something to be gotten through.

TWO KINDS OF ACTORS

There probably have always been two basic approaches to acting. The first of these is given several names: external, presentational, or style acting. The second is called internal, representational, or method acting. The fundamental difference between the two is that the first starts with the outward appearance of an individual or character and then works inward, and the second starts at the core of the role and the actor's identification with the character and then moves outward to gesture, attitude, and such concerns as manners. Such great English schools of acting as the Royal Shakespeare Company and such famous actors as Anthony Hopkins, John Gielgud, and Lawrence Olivier are all proponents of the classical, stylistic, external approach to acting. Olivier was particularly outspoken in his defense of his classical training, and there are many stories of English impatience with American "method" actors. For example, Gielgud has spoken of working with a young Marlon Brando on the set of the movie, *Julius Caesar* . He felt that Brando was a wonderfully talented young man who had no background for the role he was attempting to play (Marc Anthony). This was seen in his lack of self-

Olivier as Hamlet

Olivier in
A Flea in Her Ear

assurance about diction, handling verse, period mannerisms, and other aspects of the character that any well-trained young actor in England would have brought to such a role.

As for the other school of acting. the internal approach, the names one associates with it are the great Stanislavski, Michael Chekhov, America's Lee Strasberg, and such actors as Joanne Woodward, Anthony Quinn, and James Dean. As you move away from the classics and examine performances of modern realistic and naturalistic plays, Americans who are products of this type of training compare very favorably with their English compatriots. One of the attributes of the so-called method is that it creates actors of great individuality and range. The actors are taught to use personal emotional experiences to inform the feelings of a character they are playing; or, when this is not possible, to use Stanislavski's "Magic If." This technique allows actors to imagine what it would be like to live out certain scenarios in the absence of direct experience. Through the use of these approaches and others the well-trained actors are capable of expressing great truth and force in a variety of roles.

Although Olivier protested that the method actor will still be trying to find his character when the play closes, he himself obviously used a similar method. It was seen in such roles as Lear and Othello, which he did again and again during his career. By repeating these roles, he not only experienced audience reactions to his work but also internalized the work he was doing on them on a deeper and deeper level. Probably the argument between these two approaches becomes academic when we are dealing with performers like Olivier and Anthony Quinn. In one famous instance, they worked together in a production of *Becket* , on

Broadway (1960) and were remarkably successful in matching their acting styles.

It is our feeling that the internal or method approach has special applicability to teachers. As already described, it operates on a highly personal level and allows the individual to develop his or her special characteristics and strengths. It does not stress conformity. It doesn't prescribe the way a teacher should behave or look. After you have a grasp on the fundamentals, you may want to deal with such externals as your appearance, but this isn't your central concern: knowing who you are, how you come across, how to project honesty and sub-text, and how to use variety in shaping your performance.

THE PRESSURES OF PERFORMANCE

Another striking parallel between acting and teaching is the fact of performance. I wonder how many teachers have considered the fact that a semester-long course, with its typical schedule of forty-five lectures, is the equivalent of the run of a fairly popular play? We all know about the opening lecture "jitters" and the mid-semester sag. Perhaps we also share certain physical symptoms of dealing with classes: sore neck muscles, raspy throat, and a sense of lethargy or nervousness.   Actors also face these problems. In another chapter, we'll describe a regimen for keeping yourself in shape for teaching. We'll also introduce suggestions of how to use your voice as a strong and expressive instrument, whether for a small seminar or a large class.

The analogy is frightening real for many of us. There are both actors and teachers who will flock to the drugstores when an effective and harmless pill is invented which will control stage-fright. However, I would have strong reservations about the use of any such remedy. Stage fright, also known as "excessive concern about performance," should not only be controlled but appreciated. It helps us to do better. The truth is that teaching is special and lecturing is difficult. Generally, the more you attempt, the more difficult the opening moments will be. Compare it to an athlete's performance. A runner's fear of failure is translated not only into nausea but also the production of adrenalin: a necessity. Without it, most of us would lack the necessary metabolism for competition.

Exercise is one of the ways to prepare for this pressure. The types of exercises I will be suggesting to you are those which I have found to be most useful with actors. These involve flexing and stretching maneuvers which can be done in one's own office before going into the classroom. The vocalizing exercises I will suggest may require you to close your door, but can be done without a piano. We will have much more to say about these matters, because they are a very important part of your preparation for the reality of the classroom.

HONESTY AND SUB-TEXT

What we intend to do in the next several chapters is to teach you the fundamental techniques used by internal or method actors. Much of acting is behavioral, and it involves endless repetition and rehearsal until it is natural or comfortable. If you were enrolled in my acting class, I would first teach you HONESTY. This is not simply a matter of learning how to say what you believe. It also means to project the emotion and to vary this projection according to the size and attitude of your audience. Honesty in the theatre is both belief and technique. This shouldn't make it dishonest or manipulative. I would be disingenuous if I protested that awareness of how I am coming across somehow subverts the truthfulness of my communication. If we see a politician on television and feel that he is coming across to us as sincere and honest, we cannot be so naive as to think that he is unaware of the effect he is having on us. If it is an important address, there are probably assistants standing by, ready to comment on his speech as soon is he is done. Through them and through polls, viewing of tapes, and other types of formal and informal feedback, he is constantly developing and monitoring the impression he makes. This is precisely what actors do. At first it is a director who guides this process, then fellow actors, perhaps the stage-manager for a long-running show, and always the audiences, night after night and matinee after matinee. For an intelligent performer it is a crucial process. An actor's livelihood and career satisfaction depends on it. So does a teacher's.

Another technique to be mastered by actors is that of SUB-TEXT. By this we mean those types of communication, particularly verbal, in which indirection is used. The character says one thing but means another, and it is the actor's task to make this clear to the audience. Some forms of sub-text or indirection are familiar to all of us. For example, humor often takes this form. We may exaggerate or minimize for comic effect. We may use paradox or sarcasm. Every one of these forms of address is sub-textual and demands careful attention on the part of the performer in order that it be communicated for what it really is: the character is saying one thing but means another. Our language and culture use sub-text constantly. For one thing, it allows us to at least double our vocabulary of words and gestures. Sometimes an actor becomes famous for a particularly strong example of this sort of communication. In most cases we have to understand the context, as in the case of this fragment of dialogue and behavior which was the personal signature of the comic Jack Benny. He played the role of a skin-flint for years on radio and later on television. The moment goes like this: his character feels a gun in his back, and then the mugger says,

> MUGGER: Your money or your life!
> BENNY: (A long pause during which he crosses his
> arms, hands on chin, and seems to think it over)

Jack Benny

14

Well-l-l-l . . .

An actor or a teacher might want to experiment with playing
a role for effect. In Gilbert Highet's *The Immortal Profession,,* he
tells many stories about the legendary Kittredge of Harvard, a man
who appeared arrogant and demanding in his classroom, but
whose students knew it was a pose. It was a form of SUB-TEXT,
probably used to make them work harder.

THE NEED FOR VARIETY

VARIETY is crucial in the classroom as well as on the stage.
The skillful actor will emphasize those contrasting elements of a
role which make the character more interesting. By analogy, a
teacher will want to balance honesty with sub-text to create variety.
In the chapter on playwriting, I will suggest other types of variety
which can become parts of the presentation, but there is another
approach which should be mentioned here.

It would be an excellent exercise for every teacher to prepare a
special lecture, perhaps one given at the end of the term for the
teacher's most popular course. I've heard of a professor of
astronomy at an Ivy League university who had just such a special
lecture which he delivered each semester in the introductory
course. Against a background of special effects and music, wearing
a dazzlingly white suit for the occasion, he would deliver a
memorized script on the wonders of the universe. He seemed to
really enjoy the over-ripeness of the production he had created. As
the hour ended, he intoned his final words against the last chords
of the sound-track from *Star Wars..* It played to standing room

only. This is extreme, perhaps, but it sounds like fun for everyone.

ENERGY

In what follows there will be mention made of ENERGY. For actors and teachers it suggests a particular kind of experience one has while performing. It is not to be confused with speed of delivery, loudness, or physical tension. A skillful performer can give the impression of any one of these without using them. An actress may articulate more carefully as a substitute for volume, communicate urgency emotionally rather than by literally speeding up the words, and choreograph a violent movement so that it can be done again and again without strain or danger. ENERGY is actually PREPARATION and FOCUS.

MOVEMENT AND GESTURE

MOVEMENT and GESTURE are two more aspects of the actor's art which teachers can use. Even speech can be described as a form of gesture. Such terms as ease and eloquence used to describe a person's communication suggest this aspect of speech. "Body language" is yet another concept which I will explore.

These are all techniques and concepts used by actors which I believe can be used by teachers as the means to improve their own skills and understandings. A key concern of this study, however, is not only to explain this approach but also give you the means to criticize your own communication and improve your classroom performance. In my acting classes, I not only assign scenes for the students to prepare but I insist they learn how to be a good audience for one another. This usually seems awkward to them at the beginning. They may tend to gloss over one another's weaknesses out of kindness or to ensure a payback when they go before the class. However, they gradually come to realize that what they see and report honestly is invaluable to fellow performers. They become the best of audiences, recalling earlier failures and successes, and ready to honestly react to new efforts. Obviously teachers need workshops and seminars on teaching to create the equivalent of this ideal situation, but there is another technique available for self-improvement: learning how to read their audience's reactions.

LEARNING TO BECOME ONE'S OWN CRITIC

An actor who cannot make adjustments during performance to the audience's needs is not effective. Large changes may not be appropriate in a performance because plays are cooperative activities which have been rehearsed beforehand with cast and crew. Even in a one-character play there may be problems in the coordination of light and sound with the actor's performance which rule out radical changes during performance. However, such adaptations may be done in follow-up rehearsals. But raising one's voice to be heard, picking up a prop which has fallen, or adjusting to interruptions for applause or laughter are permissable, even necessary.

The teacher has much greater latitude in this. Not only is the script your own, but even the properties, costume, lighting, and environment are yours, unless you are making extensive use of slides or an overhead projector. What you need to develop is skill with SPLIT-FOCUS: the ability to lecture and at the same time monitor your audience's reactions. Who's fidgetting in the back row? Is there more coughing than there should be this time of year? Are they drifting away? And when you come back from checking them to checking yourself, are you bored as well? A spell-binding teacher might want to be aware when her entranced class stops taking notes. We must learn to judge how a particular remark or attitude works. Certainly, teachers can use evaluations and tests to judge our effectivenness over the longer run, but I want you to share the actor's desire to know how it is going moment to moment. It is not difficult to learn how to use SPLIT-FOCUS, and the technique is invaluable.

There are many theories about how it is actually done. Some actors insist that they do it simultaneously: they are involved in playing a role and at the same moment they are aware of how it is going across. Some claim that it is like eye-blinks. One moment you're doing the character and the next you're watching the house. Perhaps it will help us to think of communicating with an audience as taking the form of a triangle. You and your audience are the two base angles and your awareness of what's going on is the apex. When you are the slightly removed observer, you can note how much time is left, whether the class understands your line of argument, and whether you should ease up and try some humor at this moment.

Compare teaching or acting to the party game in which guests are given the name of a famous person which is pinned on their backs. It's against the rules of the game to ask someone who you are or to back up to a mirror when no one is watching. You play the game by asking questions about who you are, while the other players are trying to learn their own identities. If this were an accurate analogy to a career in teaching, your tag and theirs would constantly change. For example, you are getting older, your weight has changed, you have a new reputation, or a new haircut. Clearly, what you are learning about yourself will change how you communicate as a teacher.

Learning how to use this technique, as with most of those I will discuss in the following chapters, will take time and practice. I assume, however, that you are committed to teaching over the long haul. There will be successes and disappointments with individuals and classes, but the real skill, I believe, is not in arriving at a particular formula for success but lies in developing sensitivity and flexibility to the reality of one's self and one's audiences. A great actor, furthermore, doesn't wish to repeat the same role even though it brings fame and fortune. As Stanislavski put it, the first thing an actor should do after completing a role is to clear it from his mind and be completely open to the next role.

This is not the way many theorists feel we should improve our teaching or communication skills. I generally object to those approaches which describe what I would call surface effects. The tendency of these theorists to confuse detail with meaning reminds me of a story of the English humorist Stephen Potter. He told about a duffer who was playing golf with an expert. It was the duffer's intention to win by any means, so each time his opponent drove down a fairway or swung for the green, he winced. They were good shots, but he winced. The other man finally asks what's wrong. At this, the duffer grudgingly admits that his companion has a problem. Potter's gamesman takes out an elaborate chart to show the expert how to improve his swing. It is a life-size figure of a golfer caught mid-swing with the skin removed and all of the muscles exposed and labelled. The gamesman then proceeds to explain what's wrong with the man's stroke. Would this help you?

There is a tendency in some literature on this matter to describe what happens and how to correct it in terms of detail, not organizing principle, and to suggest a standard model rather than to accept individual differences. What I am saying would be anathema to people who would rather hear a trained speaker read a poem than hear a less polished reading by the man who wrote it. Haven't we all known teachers we admired who were careless about their appearance or had mannerisms which made us cringe the first time we met them? But they were wonderful as well as human. One powerful teacher I recall was confined to a wheelchair. Another had a lisp. But both communicated what they felt and knew with considerable skill. Think, in terms of acting, of those actors and actresses who are favorites not because of their appearance and attractive manner but because they have created a range of memorable characters and, perhaps, look like people we know.

A common problem early on in our acting classes, which I take pains to correct immediately, is the tendency on the part of some students to criticize a gesture, a phrase, an attitude which strikes them as wrong. Instead, I try to get them to analyze one another's work on the basis of overall intention, larger objectives, and feeling for the character and the relationship with other characters. Surface details should flow from these, and it is probably impossible to correct the myriad of problems which can originate in such mistaken perceptions of a role. By the way, it wasn't too many years ago that the adjective "actorish" was used to describe behavior which was flambuoyant, affected, or hammy. Nowadays it seems to have lost much of its meaning as I watch the public admiring performances by actors who are careful to delineate each role they play and strive for truthfulness in their portrayals.

CONCLUSION

Some last thoughts. There are a great many texts and articles, even training programs, in which people are "shaped" to meet a particular ideal. We all know about earlier theories of communication behavior which suggested that there were accepted ways to "sign" feelings. Nowhere in what follows will you find a list of things to do, faces to make, an attitude to carry from situation to situation. Probably the distinguishing feature of the best-known performances of the role of Hamlet has been the enormous differences among the actors playing the role. This consisted of what they brought to the part, and how they interpreted it. Think of the differences between a Mel Gibson and a Laurence Olivier, Richard Chamberlain and Alec Guinness in terms of the roles they have played and the qualities they bring to a part. They've all played the Prince of Denmark.

Each of us has some physical characteristic which we wish to control or remove, but we should strive to be what we are, and as effectively as possible. If we learn how to judge how we are communicating and learn how to adjust our behavior even during a presentation, then we are well on our way to effective teaching.

This, then, is what we are about. In the following chapters I will discuss the various techniques used by actors, the relationship of script to actor and lecture to teacher, and develop our analogy between actors and teachers. In the course of what follows, I will discuss the physical aspects of performance (body and voice), the uses of honesty and sub-text, self-correction and the development of split-focus, and describe the characteristics of our profession and teachers I have known in the past in anecdote and story.

Remember that we are dealing with lecturing, teaching seminars, and doing group presentations as important and potentially pressure-filled situations. There will be nothing in this text about how to sublimate this tension. Rather I will be talking about how to adjust to it, make the most of it, and be stimulated by it. There are many stories about the stage-fright problems of a Paul Muni or Jussi Björling. In a biography she wrote after his death, Muni's wife told of the severe stage-fright which afflicted her husband throughout his life. Bjorling was always violently ill before a concert and treated it as a payment he had to make for the work he did and the talent he

Mel Gibson in
The Road Warrior

was given. They are not the model I have in mind, but I am not going to avoid the problem. A performer without a healthy appreciation for the horrors of running into a hostile audience, losing one's place in an important lecture, or committing an inadvertant blunder has no respect for the potential of the situation. Without this you may be like those performers we've all known who assured us before opening night that it was going to be easy, we shouldn't worry, and then proceeded to demonstrate to the audience that the role was boring.

---

[1]Philip W. Jackson, "The Way Teaching Is," in Contemporary Thought on Teaching," ed. Ronald T. Hayman (Englewood Cliffs, New Jersey: Prentice-Hall, Inc., 1971), p.6.

CHAPTER 2
ACTORS AND ACTING

К. С. СТАНИСЛАВСКИЙ (1863—1938)

CHAPTER 2: ACTORS AND ACTING

Both teacher and actor share the same goal: the communication of ideas and feelings to an audience. The playwright gives the actor a character through whom to present these. An actor's objective is to create a believable character in order to facilitate this conveyance. Teachers usually do not work through a character. Their presentations are more direct. Nevertheless, the end is the same: to touch the audience with ideas and feelings. Interestingly, actors have developed techniques in communication that we as teachers can utilize.

As already noted in the introduction, over the years two main approaches to creating a character have developed: the external and internal. No matter which approach is taken, there is a common initial step in the analysis of the character. One has to know a character before attempting to bring it to life. As I heard Richard Digby Day, Director of England's Nottingham Playhouse, tell his cast as they rehearsed Shakespeare's *Taming of the Shrew* . " Know the map of your part, then free yourself to play the role moment to moment."[1] The American actor, Hume Cronyn, has noted the danger of a partially realized process: "Whenever there is a vacuum in the actor's thinking, it will be filled with a cliché."[2] Constantin Stanislavski (1863-1938), the noted Russian actor, director, and teacher of acting, also warned actors of the need to know their characters and avoid stock answers: "The very worst fact is that clichés will fill up every empty spot in a role, which is not already filled with living feeling. Moreover, they often rush in ahead of feeling, and bar the road; that is why an actor must protect himself most conscientiously against such

(Opposite) Constantin Stanislavski (1863-1938)

devices. And this is true of even gifted actors, capable of true creativeness."[3]

An examination of the analytical process the actor uses should provide insights for teachers. For example, an important premise for the actor's character analysis is that a grasp of the character's total personality will enable the actor to play each moment of the character's life on stage with greater perception. If we as teachers have a comprehensive grasp of the purpose of the entire lecture, we will be better able to deliver each section of our presentation. Furthermore, as Uta Hagen reminds us in her book on acting, *Respect for Acting* : "All the tedious research is worth one inspired moment."[4]

BODY LANGUAGE

The first step in the actor's analysis is to read the play for a clear understanding of the plot. Actors are usually eye-minded and tend to visualize the play as they read it. Settings will appear in the actor's mind, as will the characters who populate the action. These initial, unsolicited images may often influence the actor's development of a character. Imagined details of a character's appearance or behavior may find their way into an actor's final portrayal.

Once actors have a grasp of what is happening in a play, they are ready to concentrate on the role they are playing. Playwrights create characters on a number of levels and the actor wants to determine how these levels function within the character. Most easily observable is probably the physical level. The actor will ask, "What does the playwright tell me about the physical nature of this character?" It is not unusual for the author to provide descriptions of the character's appearance and behavior. This is often given before the first speech.

A wonderful example of this use of description is to be found in the opening of Arthur Miller's *Death of a Salesman:* "[Willy Loman] is past sixty years of age, dressed quietly. Even as he crosses the stage to the doorway of the house, his exhaustion is apparent."[5] An actor has a starting point for how to portray the character physically. An age is given and an attitude is implied. The words "dressed quietly" and "exhaustion" leap out at you, and the actor's understanding and experimentation has begun. In addition to the playwright's physical description of character, the actor will search actions for clues to his physical nature. The character George in Steinbeck's *Of Mice and Men* easily crushes Curly's hand when they meet, immediately establishing in this one action two very important facts about the character crucial to the play: George is enormously strong, but he lacks understanding of how this affects others.

What can the actor's examination of the character's physical reality suggest to us as teachers? We too can benefit from an examination of the physical presence we project to our students. Are we overbearing? Too relaxed? Are our bodies communicating what we want them to? The actor wants a thorough understanding of what must be communicated physically before attempting to find the means to project it. We too can benefit from asking ourselves what we want our bodies to convey. "It's the first day of classes and I'm as excited as you." "It was a rough examination, you did well, and now it's time to relax a bit before we forge ahead." These are two different situations in which our attitudes may be served by contrasting body styles.

THE PSYCHOLOGICAL APPROACH

Actors will tell you that the next most important level on which their characters exist is the psychological one. They examine the script carefully to determine what emotions their characters experience and how they project them. Actors are obsessed with a desire to know their characters' objectives. What controls or drives them as people? What is the overall objective that is pulling a character through the whole play (Stanislavski's super objective)? Hamlet's super objective is most often identified as his the desire to avenge his father's death. What are the specific objectives that the actor needs to be aware of in each scene relating to this super objective, and what is it he faces in each scene? While revenge may be Hamlet overall objective, his immediate objective may be to determine his uncle's guilt, to establish the fact that Polonius is spying on him, or break his ties with Ophelia. Taking this objectifying process down to its basics may involve breaking even lines and the smallest action into units of thought. The actor asks himself, what do I mean when I say "To be or not to be that is the question," "the readiness is all," or "Get thee to a nunnery"?

Stanislavski sums up the rationale for the actor's examination of the role in these succinct terms: "Whatever happens on stage must be for a purpose . . . If an action has no inner foundation, it cannot hold your [the audience's] attention."[6] So it is with teachers, as well. What is the super-objective of your lecture? Let's say it is to convey Mendel's contributions to science. What is the specific objective of your introductory comments? You reply, to arouse their interest. After this objective has been achieved, your next objective may be to lay out the broad outlines of your treatment of the subject, then to get down to specifics. But interspersed with this progress may be units whose specific objectives are to surprise them with an entertaining aspect of the material or test their understanding to that point. Only after actors and teachers understand their objectives can they effectively add feelings to their presentations and deal with the physical realization of their performance.

In addition to physical and psychological concerns, playwrights move on to develop a character's encompassing psychological and emotional existence on stage. It is at this point that the two main approaches to creating a character diverge. The internal method is based on the belief that it is necessary for the actor to experience the emotion being projected. The argument goes that you cannot show an audience what you do not, to some degree, feel yourself. Sir Laurence Olivier, who was generally considered as belonging to the other school of acting, acknowledged this necessity:

So if you are playing a part you must ask yourself what kind of a man he was. Then, when you know, you must somehow be that man — not just the part that shows in the role, but the whole of the man, his whole mind, so what you actually reveal in the role is real and right because in your mind you have got the whole underlying man real and right. It's your sense of the realness of people which gives your rightness about them when you act. . . Oh, God, yes, you have to feel it to do it. The suffering, the passion, the bitterness, you've got to feel them. And it takes something out of you and puts something in, as all emotional experiences do.[7]

The external approach, however, is rooted in the concept that the audience is most interested in what it sees. It seeks to de-emphasize what the actor is experiencing. Appearance will reflect the reality. However, the passage from Olivier's biography which I have just noted gives the lie to easy generalizations about the two schools of training. Obviously not all external actors avoid inner feelings and not all internal actors avoid the craft of managing appearances. As for the latter, many are shrewd imitators of accents, manners, and attitudes. Dustin Hoffman's work in the movie *Rainman* combined both approaches. He had explored his character's condition and had found ways to portray to that most critical of all observers, the motion picture camera. The final word from Olivier is that he objects to an acting technique which when taken too seriously prevents the actor from getting his character on stage in time for opening night

Ideally the internal actor finds the emotional basis for his character and then works through it in the time allotted for rehearsals. What the actor does at the outset, when attempting to experience the emotions of a role, is to use emotional recall or another technique called the "Magic If." Both were described and developed by Constantin Stanislavski, who is the single most important promulgator of this approach to acting.

When using emotional recall, actors delve into their own pasts to find experiences which provoke the same feelings their characters are feeling. Sometimes you may find identical experiences, but there will be times that you must "build bridges," as Uta Hagen puts it, between what you have experienced and what the character is going through. Imagine that you are portraying Romeo in *Romeo and Juliet.* Your character has to show the excitement, the exhilaration of first love. The character's words cannot keep pace with his feelings. His heart is beating faster than his lips and tongue can move. It is the famous balcony scene! But, despite the fame and uniqueness of this moment from the play, the actor has the task of recalling his own "first balcony scene," though it may have taken place on a porch or in the family livingroom and in the mundane accents of everyday life. Certain elements will come back more readily than others. His sweetheart might have been wearing a particular dress or her face had a glow. These might be the key. You then remember the perfume she was wearing that night. A building process has begun which could lead the actor to literally recall the tone of the girl's voice and small details of the actual environment which hadn't been thought of for years. What is important in this whole process of recollection is that as his own "balcony" scene comes back, so do the specific emotions which were felt then. Emotions do not exist in a vacuum.

Though it was formalized in modern times by Stanislavski, emotional memory can be traced back to classical times. In his book, *The Length and Depth of Acting,* Edwin Duerr retells the story of Polus of Aegina, a great actor of his time, who in a scene in which he was to remove the ashes of Orestes from a tomb and grieve over them, actually used the ashes of his own son and "embraced them as if they were those of Orestes, and filled the whole place, not with the appearance and imitation of sorrow, but with genuine grief and unfeigned lamentation."[8] We would want to caution an actor nowadays to go through this experience in rehearsal, in order to purify and control the emotion. For an audience one is art but the former may seem like eavesdropping. And a danger with the method, or internal acting, is that there can be too much self-absorption, a failure to realize the essential difference between theatre and reality, and ultimately a lack of understanding of the audience's needs.

I have heard about a young, inexperienced actress who was playing in a professional production and thrilled to hear, one night, that John Gielgud, the actor-director, was in the audience. Her excitement and understandable desire to do well led her to feel things about her character that she had never felt before. In one emotional scene she wept for the first time, with real sorrow. Afterwards, she eagerly awaited Sir John's visit backstage, expecting praise for a role she had never before felt so deeply. He did finally appear and gave her a rather perfunctory compliment, then sensing that she expected more, he turned at the door and said, "Next time let your audience do the crying, my dear."

It wasn't meant literally, of course, but it's a fact of the stage. Emotion too centered in the actor never seems to get out to an audience. It's uncomfortable for us. We don't want to watch a real father handling a real son's ashes in eight performances a week. This is why people invented theatre. Audiences understand it very well. I think of the uncounted times I have heard and seen audiences react to a dropped line or the unintended, unrehearsed stumble. I knew, but how did they? They knew exactly where theatre ended and life began.

I spoke of "building bridges." At times actors find themselves in new situations. When this happens, they begin by searching their memories for previous experiences which might be similar. The important fact is that the situation must provoke the same sort of emotion. For example, a young woman might be playing Linda Loman, Willy's wife, in a college production of *Death of a*

Salesman. In the scene being rehearsed, the character is feeling a deep sense of grief and anger at her husband's death, which was a suicide. It is conceivable that a college student might not have experienced the death of a loved one. However, she can think of an event that brought on the twin emotions of loss and anger. She may not want to say what this is, because it might not be understood, and it is clearly no one else's business. What matters is that it yields the results the actress and the director want. How does this technique fit into the rehearsal process? Many actors prefer to go through these exercises in private. Directors working with trained actors will often suggest a behavior and then leave it to their actors to discover the solution on their own.

There is a story about Lee J. Cobb preparing the role of Willy Loman in its premiere production. One of the supporting actors noted that in the early weeks of rehearsal Cobb seemed remote, divorced from the rest of them. The weeks of preparation were rushing by and the star was mumbling his lines, refusing to play off other characters, and generally alarming everyone with his isolation. Then one morning, this actor wrote, there was a stranger who appeared on the stage with them for that day's rehearsal and his name was Willy Loman, in the person of Lee J. Cobb.

Certainly there are instances, even in the professional theatre, when a director or another actor will help you find your role. Questions relevant to the situation might help. "How old were you when your friend moved away?" "How long had you been friends?" "Where were you and what were you doing when you found out she was moving?" The questions and presence of the questioner gives the actor immediate feedback as to the quality of the emotion being projected.

Actors using emotion memory are always cautioned to keep in mind the necessity for maintaining control. Acting is a disciplined art. Aside from the danger of self-indulgence, already noted, there is also the problem of jeopardizing one's ability to proceed to the scene's next moment. If I permit myself to feel the pain or joy too deeply, I may not be ready to respond when the playwright commands me to follow the next change in character or plot.

Another story of actors and their problems with difficult roles is appropriate here. Several years ago I saw a scene from *Come Back, Little Sheba* done in a beginning acting class. Doc, an alcoholic, returns home in a drunken rage. He and his wife, Lola, argue and then he chases her, hatchet in hand. During the chase it became clear to the class that the actor playing Doc was not in control of his emotions. A few of the swipes he was taking with the weapon were too close and too intentional. But the scene ended and we all drew a sigh of relief. The actor admitted in the subsequent discussion that he had lost control, and we in turn

Lee J. Cobb as Willy Loman in Death of A Salesman

reported to him that our whole concern had been for the actress, not the character she was portraying. We had totally divorced ourselves from the characters and scene because of his behavior. The lesson for all of us was that both the emotion and the control must be found beforehand.

As one can imagine, the initial use of emotional memory can be time-consuming. However, the rehearsal environment is usually designed to allow for this, maximizing the actor's time for exploration and interaction with both the director and other actors. Once found, most actors can recall the emotion as needed. Eventually, through repetition and concentration, the lines and actions become magnets that pull the required response from the actor almost spontaneously.

Emotion memory strikes us as being a potentially meaningful tool for teachers. There may be a number of reasons why we are not projecting the proper emotion in our lectures. It may be the end of the semester and we are exhausted. Ironically, our students may feel the same way, making it even more difficult for them to accept our attitude. Taking our cue from what we may know about acting, we can use emotion memory to recall, perhaps, the first time we delivered today's lecture or our enthusiasm and excitement when we first experienced the material to be presented. We can recapture these feelings before we step into the class.

Here's another situation. The results of the first examination were poor. I feel required to reprimand my students, but years of teaching have made it impossible to find the proper level of indignation. After years at this school, I make excuses for them which are self-fulfilling. But this time I realize the need for a tough reaction. So I may bring back to mind an incident which elicited our stern reaction in a completely different situation and use this as the tone for our reprimand. It would be best if we could remember a class which really had disappointed us to the point of anger, but we may have to settle on something close: a child or a pet that should have known better but destroyed a book or a pair of shoes.

THE MAGIC IF

The "Magic If" is the other important tool actors use when they are working on the projection of inner emotion. When confronted with the need to play an emotion with which she is having difficulty, an actress might ask herself the question, "What would I feel if I were the person in the situation?" "If I were Juliet, how would I respond to the voice in the darkness below?" "If I were Linda, how would I feel standing beside Willy's grave after the others have left?" Obviously, the use of the "Magic If" demands that the actor possess a vivid enough imagination to transport herself into another person. Calling on a child's ability for make-believe, the actor pretends to be the other person. The process demands that actors step away from themselves. Once they start experiencing the world through Romeo's or Juliet's eyes, and not their own, they find they can project the required emotions. Having skill with emotional recall helps this process, but so does the protection of the rehearsal situation, in which actors can pretend to have an emotion until it begins to be real. Some actors will carry experimentation with the "Magic If" outside the rehearsal. They might eat a meal, walk through a park, or watch a sunset in the persona of their character. The "Magic If," which is truly one of an actor's most valuable tools, can be used to place a character in any emotional situation.

How might it be used in a teaching situation? We can imaginatively project ourselves into the emotion that any situation requires. Let's imagine that it's the beginning of the semester and we notice several students talking during our presentation. It is distracting, but years of teaching have diluted the anger this behavior used to elicit. We realize, however, that if this interference isn't stopped, it will encourage others to follow suit or at least to be distracted from the main business of the class. We will conjure up the necessary anger by the use of the "Magic If." "What if I were really upset by these students?" "How would I feel?" The technique releases feelings which are familiar but dormant. The entire class is shocked by the "reasoned" force of my outburst. On one occasion that I remember there was such a couple in the rear of the room and I found the appropriate emotional response. I looked them in the eye and said with more feeling than I felt, "If you believe that your conversation is more important than the class' right to hear what the teacher has to say about this topic, then I must ask you to leave the classroom and take it out into the hall."

An equally demanding situation that demonstrates the classroom use of the "Magic If" is the first lecture of the semester. Let's imagine a situation in which we are well prepared and are convinced of the validity of what we want to say in our introduction of the material. What is lacking is a sense of confidence which seems to have abandoned us this morning. We know, intellectually, that our confidence will build during the year, but this is today and we're not looking forward to the next hour. The "Magic If" prompts me to say, "How would I feel if I had met with this class successfully a dozen times before?" I focus on this feeling, let it fill me, and then step into the classroom.

MICHAEL CHEKHOV

In his book *To The Actor,* Michael Chekhov suggests an additional technique that can aid the actor in projecting emotion. He calls for the actor to envision his character, to actually see him acting. In her mind's eye, the actress playing Amanda in Tennessee Williams' *The Glass Menagerie* sees herself questioning her daughter, Laura, about the classes at the business school. She sees the pain in Amanda's face and body as she tells Laura of going to the teacher of the typing class, expecting a report on her daughter's progress, only to learn that she attended once and never returned. She imagines the character asking where her daughter has been spending her time since she left school? Chekhov suggests that looking at the image of your character can awaken in you "those feelings, emotions and will impulses so necessary to your performances of the character."[9] In this instance, the actress' imagination unlocks the feelings of pain and anger within her which the role demands she feel during the play. We might remember Albert Einstein's dictum: "Imagination is more important than knowledge." This is particularly true for actors.

As teachers we can "picture" ourselves teaching. We might see the excitement we are creating in the students as we reach the key point in a favorite lecture. We might note the way we pick up our intensity when their attention seems to wander. We see ourselves telling a joke, remembering not to laugh first at our own humor. Perhaps, at the same time, Chekhov's suggestion is working. We are beginning to feel the emotions our imagination is picturing.

How does the actor who is using this internal approach deal with the physical realization of the character? Basically, the internal actor believes that the externalization of the emotion will flow naturally from the feeling of it. "If I feel it, I will show it." Of course if actors are playing someone considerably older or with marked physical characteristics, they must consciously adapt their bodies and manners of movement to that of the character. One way to do this which is consistent with the theory of internal acting is to find a cause for the new behavior. A young woman asked to play an aging character might create the stiffness of joints by immobilizing her knees with wrappings. But she has also observed a crab-like walk used by several older women she has known. She reasons that this may not be caused entirely by the stiffness of the knee joints which she is simulating. What if it is also a response to a fear of falling, perhaps the terror of a shattered bone which will not heal and will mean spending the rest of her life bedridden? Now our actress has found the physical and emotional basis for a walk which she will use in rehearsals until it feels natural .

MORE ABOUT EXTERNAL ACTORS

This is a good point at which to consider the approach to acting made by the external actor. As previously noted, the analysis of character done at the beginning of the rehearsal period is the same with both approaches: an identical survey of attitudes, traits, and objectives. Remember that the external actor's priority at this point is the external manifestations of the character. The good external actor is a student of human nature. One must not equate the word "external" with the notion of "superficial." "Observation" becomes an operative term in the process which follows. As Laurence Olivier noted, "I usually collect a lot of details, a lot of characteristics, and find a creature swimming around in them."[10]

The skilled external actor is an astute observer searching out various physical manifestations of a given emotion so that it may be called back and duplicated when needed. During rehearsals these external qualities are adapted to fit the character. A director might note that two actors are using the same signals for a given emotion and correct this. Robert Goulet's first major Broadway role was opposite Richard Burton in the musical *Camelot.* Because he was not a trained actor, he was petrified, and spent a great deal of time watching Richard Burton for clues on how to handle himself. Several days into the rehearsal period Burton pulled him aside. The gist of what he said to Goulet was, 'look, will you kindly pick one of the characters I've been inventing every night and stick with it? I'm tired of inventing new ones.'

Imagine you are playing Emily, the young girl in Thornton Wilder's *Our Town.* It is the scene in the drugstore in which George asks her to marry him. You have identified the emotion felt by your character at the peak of this scene as joyous excitement. Your research has told you that people in this condition feel elated and smile uncontrollably. They arch their eyebrows, lift their heads and shoulders. Or if you're Julie Andrews in another production standing on a hilltop in the Alps, you start spinning and singing, releasing all of this pent-up energy. The ordinary person speaks of being "up!" Some of us would call it "being on top of the world." As I list these, I begin to feel the emotion that the first scene requires and it begins to fill me. Feeling the emotion in this way is not the intention of the external approach, but it can be an important by-product.

In addition to emotion, technique is another important tool for the external actor. Simply put, technique is a standard method for the execution of a piece of behavior. The history of theatre proves that there are time-honored methods for drawing attention or speaking in such a way that you are audible to everyone but give the impression of whispering. Sometimes an actor is admired for making a difficult piece of business appear easy or bringing a sense of style to something that is very ordinary. Frank Langella, the American actor, appeared in the title role in **Dracula** on Broadway. Several times during the performance he removed his cape as he entered the scene and threw it across the room in one graceful motion. The cape would then fly through the air and land, wrapping itself perfectly around a chair. Of course this piece of "business" was the result of endless practice, but so are sitting, standing, and gesturing for the external actor. Cary Grant's behavior in his most popular films was as studiedly idiosyncratic, as David Niven's was elegant. Although I always enjoyed Sean Connery in the James Bond films, he never quite carried it off. Or so I thought. He was like an elephant in a tutu. He is not a good external actor, and probably doesn't want to be. But if you've seen him in such films as **The Hill** or **The Man Who Would be King,,** you know he's a superb internal actor.

Let me give you some further examples of the concerns of external actors. For example, imagine the part requires that I sit.

In real life I might look back at the chair as I sit down and steady myself with my hand, but the technically oriented actor, not wanting his audience to pay attention to this act, or wanting them only to note the fluidity of his movements, will find the chair with his leg and sit in one motion. F. Cowles Strickland's *The Technique of Acting* describes hundreds of such techniques.

Just as the internal actor has to be alert to keeping control of the character's feelings, the external actor has to be certain that his performance is projecting the feeling of the role. As Uta Hagen, already identified as a practitioner and teacher of internal acting, has put it for all actors: "I have found that something gets stale and dries up only when I become aware of outer effects or watching my actions rather than staying involved and truly executing them."[11]

Both schools of acting, furthermore, emphasize the need for the actor to sustain a role during the run of a show. According to the external theory of acting, an actor must be so in control of his technique that he is able to repeat his performance at the same level again and again. Helen Hayes tells the story about Olivier's performance of Othello which transcended all of the many he had given. "At the end of the play," she writes,"after his last call - with the audience still cheering - Olivier made his way to his dressing room through two lines of fellow actors who were also applauding him. He ignored them all and slammed the door." Someone knocked and called out, "What's the matter Larry? It was great!" Olivier shouted through the door, "I know it was great, damn it, but I don't know how I did it, so how can I be sure I can do it again."[12]

In conclusion, what can I say about the value of the external approach to the teacher? Obviously one should study both approaches and use the one which is more agreeable. Again, let's imagine that it is the first day of classes and despite long hours of faculty meetings and paperwork, we want very much to communicate to our new students our enthusiasm at meeting them and having this opportunity to share our interest with them. We infuse our voices and bodies with this excitement, speak with greater force and focus, and increase the scale of our gestures. Everything is orchestrated to communicate controlled excitement. And as we do this, the true emotion begins to appear. When we again turn to the blackboard, it is only for the briefest moment, because the class deserves our full attention and the board is used for amplification and clarification, not for private monologue. The process is under way. The class continues . . .

SOME ADDITIONAL TOOLS

The basic tools of actors are their bodies and voices, the so-called "instruments," and their emotions and technique. Beyond these there are a number more which are of great value: costume and make-up, properties, settings, and, for lack of a better term, "atmospheres." All of these are at least touched upon in the training of an actor and have immediate and lasting importance for a teacher.

I suspect that some clothing could be thought of as symbolic. What about the jeans, plaid shirts, and leather hats of the sixties, still worn by a few aging professors on college campuses? Another familiar costume is the three-piece suit or gray flannels and tweed jackets. When I dress up for a day at school, it is usually for another commitment, and I am somewhat disconcerted by the students' interest in how I look. Do they mean that I look different or that I look better? Haircuts also get notice as do the frequent suntans of a faculty friend who sails. We would be fooling ourselves if we didn't think costuming and make-up matter.

This leads me to a recollection of a time when I used costuming very purposefully in class. I was teaching Theatre History and the class was nervous about the examination I was scheduled to give, so I dressed and did a make-up for the occasion. I carried in the exams dressed as a *commedia dell'arte* character. Everyone had a good laugh, and they relaxed as they settled down to the work at hand, but every so often individuals would look up quizzically, as though they needed reassurance that they had really seen me do this craziness. The pay-off was both immediate and long-range. The exams were pretty good, and on final examination day, perhaps a minute after the test started, a young woman from the class who had been taking a class in

Olivier as Richard III

costuming appeared in a beautiful Elizabethan gown of her own design and manufacture. The class applauded her, she sat down, and we all got to work.

On my campus there are several teachers who take this matter of costuming and make-up one step farther. They have invented characters whom they play as part of their teaching and off-campus appearances. One is a dead-ringer for Abraham Lincoln, on whom he has done extensive research, and can put together entertaining speeches complete with Lincoln's humor, physical characteristics, and in some instances his exact opinions on the topic under discussion. The other two are both history teachers who have created characters who visit their classrooms as special guests. One of them loves to tell the story about the time that his Russian peasant, a man who lived before 1917, visited the classroom, complete with accent, costume, make-up, and attitudes. At the close of his visit, a young woman in the class came up to him and said, "Mr. Vladimir, would you please tell Professor Long that I can't make that appointment this afternoon?"

The second tool for an actor and teacher is the use of properties. Insecure actors are always reaching for a cigarette. If they are supposed to be reading a book during the scene, they become speed readers, or that actor with the watch fob wears the audience out checking time. However, those of us who were lucky saw one of the great pieces of property utilization when we saw either Pearl Bailey or Carol Channing do the dumpling-eating scene in *Hello, Dolly*. What about the way Marlon Brando used his wheel-chair in *The Men* or his handling of the shabby jewelry from Blanch's trunk in *A Streetcar Named Desire?* Think of the challenge for an actor playing Volpone in the scene in which he fondles his precious gold pieces, or Queeg's unconscious rattling of the ball-bearings he always carries with him when he testifies in *The Caine Mutiny Court Martial.* A favorite Hitchcock television episode was the one about the woman who killed her husband with a frozen leg of lamb and then destroyed the evidence by having the police inspector to dinner. Remember it?

In acting, we speak of the psychological gesture, but well-handled properties have the capacity to become psychological and physical extensions of the actor. There does seem to be one *caveat,* however. Don't let them take over; don't let them become the message. In teaching, the overhead projector and slide carousel are useful properties unless the user allows them to replace her as the center of focus. As a senior art professor once told me, never compete with a visual. Some professors I know have learned how to manage this challenge. One used very few slides and a daylight screen, which allowed him to hold center stage. The other showed slides at the end of the class as amplification and corroboration of the lecture he had just given.

What can you do with a piece of chalk? Unless you were a Darwin or Agazziz, who according to Gilbert Highet, were both men with great artistic skill and could talk and draw and marry the two right under the eyes of their fascinated classes; unless you were they, you had better do your drawing beforehand or use a hand-out. With all too many of us the blackboard becomes a giant navel for personal contemplation. What do you do with chalk? I have heard tales, probably invented, of professors who keep their class's attention by accurately winging bits of chalk at talkers. This reminds me of a dear friend who had a nervous mannerism, an inadvertant use of props. Because he had come to teaching late in life, after a successful career as a manufacturer, it was obvious to him how truly difficult it was to teach. He dealt with this by knowing his subject matter and treating his students like friends, but he was still nervous. It showed in his habit of keeping a hand in his pocket and jangling his coins. One day he became deeply involved in a class discussion and he couldn't wait to get his hand out to gesture as he made a point. Out came a handful of coins and, as his arm did a sweeping gesture, he scattered them over his audience. I wish I could have seen their expressions. Their surprise must have been wonderful to see, almost worth his embarrassment?

I have always believed that highschool science teachers are the most effective professionals, because they are constantly proving the point that one good experiment is worth hours of dry lecturing. Even college level classes can be exciting. The best use of props I've heard of lately was the anatomy professor who demonstrates the manner in which we produce sound by bringing in a sheep's larynx and connecting it to a compressor and air hose. It actually sounded like a sheep.

There isn't a professional actor in the world who would willingly go on stage without first taking a walk about the stage on which he is about to perform. Many carry this to an extreme. I recall two young women who were appearing in my production of *Mother Courage* . They asked permission to live in the wagon used on stage, for several days. I was happy to comply. They had discovered an important fact about their two characters, Mother Courage and her daughter Kattrin. They knew the wagon was home to them and they didn't want to behave during performance in a way which would give the lie to this reality. The same girl who played Katryn endlessly practiced the acrobatic fall which her character makes from the peasant's roof, when she is shot at play's end. She was a splendid gymnast and was aware of the need to know her equipment: the roof's surface and a post which she grasped as she tumbled past. She shielded this action from the audience and each evening they gasped when they thought she had fallen directly to the stage floor.

I remember being somewhat nonplussed when I discovered how much time is spent in the professional theatre perfecting just such interactions of actors with settings and properties. Years ago, I spent an afternoon watching a famous Canadian Shakespeare company rehearsing a piece of business which involved the disappearance of a character into an open trap door. The mind boggles at the time and energy expended in the professional productions of such plays as *Noises Off* or *Sleuth*, which demand very complex stage effects. In the first, there are monumental problems with split-second timing of entrances and exits, and in the latter the actors must work with a myriad of props, most of which are dangerous.

Another matter of concern for actors in their interaction with stage settings is how to create focus or bring out emotional values. First, for an example of focus we might consider how an actor "takes" stage. With a gifted and experienced actor it is rarely as blatant as moving down center and directly addressing the audience. Our attention can be pulled anywhere on stage. In a famous nineteenth century French production of *Julius Caesar,* the opening scene with the townspeople was being played against a background of a broad sweep of steps which was topped by a colonnade. As the scene progressed, a number of prominent

Romans appeared at the top of the steps and then crossed downstage diagonally and exited down right. Our expectations of seeing Caesar would have risen with the appearance of each new group and the turning of the heads of the commoners standing closest to us. Then a final group appeared and started down, but one short, inconspicuous man remained behind for an instant. A shop-keeper turned and saw him, turned to his neighbor and remarked, "Ici Caesar." There's Caesar.

Dame Edith Evans, one of England's greatest actresses, visited Stratford, Ontario's Festival Theatre, a large and beautiful thrust stage with a large balcony and an audience which surrounds it in a 220 degree sweep. Legend has it that she went up on stage and unerringly moved to a point just in front of the balcony on the top step beneath it and just a little right of center. When she had stopped at this point she called out, "Where does one stand to get attention on this stage?"

During his years at Weimar, Goethe formalized his understanding of stagecraft into a series of rules. Among other things, he assigned emotions and proper actions to different parts of the stage. What he was imagining was a formal theatre not unlike the Japanese Noh drama in which settings and stage behavior are highly stylized. Gratefully, his ideas did not catch on, but there is still wide agreement on how things should be managed for certain effects. However, these "conventions" exist to be broken.

What about the connections to teaching? Should a teacher stand behind a lectern? Should you ever step down into the audience? Is there a magic gulf in a classroom as there is thought to be in a theatre, which separates teacher and students? I have asked these and similar questions of a number of teachers, very few of whom had any training in theatre. Most admitted after seeing one another give lectures that the position behind the lectern was somewhat inhuman. It was a point of focus, but seemed to have a negative affect on attention span. There did seem to be a "magic gulf" between the teacher and the front row of the audience. Many spoke of the energy (or strangeness) they felt when they stepped into this area and through it. Clearly their presence challenged the students in the front row and to some extent all of the students in the room. There was no consensus, however, as to whether or not it was a good idea. We agreed that teachers should think about these matters and experiment. A majority felt that the best area at the front of the typical classroom was in front of the lectern, beside the gulf, to the students' left. They all felt it was important that the blackboard be visible to everyone and if it weren't, then hand-outs should be used.

THE FINAL TOOL: ATMOSPHERICS

The final tool for the actor is what I am calling "atmospherics." Lighting and music come to mind immediately. Much of modern theatre is performed on almost empty, space stages using lighting as a powerful aesthetic tool to communicate warmth, alienation, space, closeness, romance, or stark reality. As for music, nineteenth century Parisians discovered its power in the spoken theatre when there was a government ban placed on straight drama. They turned to drama with music, which they called "melodrame." This was later corrupted into America's melodramas. But the power of music in the theatre was obvious.

Perhaps the best known extension of this use is to be found in the cinema. We are so used to its employment that it doesn't strike us as strange when the Los Angeles Symphony puts its large sound into an intimate scene. In *High Anxiety,* Mel Brooks was driving along the Pacific Highway. His character was headed toward a fateful rendezvous with his crazed therapists. It is a suspenseful moment and, sure enough, an orchestra begins to play appropriate music. It rises to a thunder, and then a bus passes his car filled with musicians busily making that music.

Could seating arrangements also be part of classroom "atmospherics"? A circle of chairs is warmer and friendlier than the usual classroom's rows. Let the room be illuminated by natural light from the windows or use the new florescents which have a reddish cast rather than the familiar cold blue. The list goes on. Perhaps we cannot adjust the lighting or play background music, but we should consider what can be done to promote certain feelings in the space being used. One of the classrooms I use is also a rehearsal space for summer shows. Whenever I come into this room, I sense the ghosts of all the shows I've worked on there and the presence of all the student actors with whom I've worked. I look at the floor and imagine I am seeing the long-erased tape lines for countless settings. Obviously this is my preferred space for teaching acting.

In his excellent book on teaching, *The Immortal Profession,* Gilbert Highet writes, "The most important part of our work is discovery and reinterpretation . . ."[13] We should always be open to new ideas about our teaching as well as about our subject area. I am contending that one rich area of inquiry for all of us can be the study of the art of acting, but there are, of course, many, many more. The major point for us is that we are involved in change and adaptation, and to use Aristotle's wonderful word, we are, ideally, in the act of "becoming."

1Richard Digby Day, Interview held in Nottingham, England, April 27,1982.

2Hume Cronyn, Interview held in Denver, Colorado, February 21,1980.

3 Constantin Stanislavski," An Actor Prepares," trans.Elizabeth Reynolds Hapgood (New York: Theatre Arts Books, 1936), p.25.

4Uta Hagen with Haskel Frankel, "Respect for Acting" (New York: Macmillan, l973), p.153.

5 Arthur Miller, "Death of A Salesman," in A TREASURY OF THE THEATRE, ed. John Gassner (New York: Holt, Rinehart and Winston, 1960), p.1063.

6Stanislavski, pp.33-41.

7John Cottrell, "Lawrence Olivier" (Englewood Cliffs, New Jersey: Prentice-Hall,1975), p.392.

8Edwin Duerr, "The Length and Depth of Acting" (Holt, Rinehart and Winston, 1962), p.36.

9Michael Chekhov, "To the Actor on the Technique of Acting" (New York: Harper and Row Publishers, 1953) p.26.

10Cottrell, p.389.

11Hagen, p.205.

12Helen Hayes with Sanford Dody, "On Reflection, An Autobiography" (Boston: Lanewood Press, Inc., 1968), p.127.

CHAPTER 3
EXERCISES

NORTH POLE
EQUATOR
SOUTH POLE
THE CENTER OF THE
ANGULAR DISTA
EAST OR WE
THE PRIME M

CHAPTER 3: EXERCISES

I have been developing the analogy of acting to teaching. There is yet another striking parallel. Teaching, like acting, involves performing and often causes all of the strains and tensions associated with performance. In doing workshops for teachers, some questions always come up early in the day and are repeated throughout: What about nervousness? What about this fatigue I often feel? What about burn-out? Even when we've been teaching competently for years, anxiety will strike unexpectedly. As a teacher myself, I know exactly what they are experiencing. I hope I don't sound facetious if I admit that I expect nervousness at the start of a semester and occasional sharp pangs even late in the year. I can unexpectedly go through everything from light-headedness, to gnawing anxiety, to unexpected physical distresses when faced with a special lecture, a grade change, or an interview with a student whose failure needs discussion but is probably a function of cramming the night before the examination. I expect these feelings to crop up. I suspect that I would really be concerned if they didn't.

The same is the case with the actors I've known. As I noted in the first chapter, the really bad ones frequently are positive that there's nothing to worry about. I believe that a certain level of anxiety and tension are necessary concomitants to performance. Furthermore, there is always the possibility of irrational stage-fright leaping full-grown at me out of the most familiar situations.

Perhaps you saw the interview with Sir Laurence Olivier, conducted a year or two before his death. He admitted he had gone through a terrible bout of stage-fright during the period when he

*(Opposite) Dr. Roger B. Culver, Professor of Astronomy, Colorado State University. (Photo: The C.S.U. **Collegian**)*

was doing *Othello*, on stage at Chichester and later in the film. There were performances when he didn't believe he could make it on stage, and when he did he was convinced that he must run to the wings, escaping the audience.

It is my belief that we must face our fears and learn to use them. Sometimes it seems to have the same fascination as a sore tooth which we know we mustn't explore with our tongue. Every Sunday, if you enjoy other people going through agony, you can watch on television the final round of a golf tournament. This has always struck me as the most terrifying of all ordinary, acceptable sports. The action is so deliberate that the temptation to anguish over your mistakes and second-guess your next move must be overwhelming. The competition is head-to-head and nerve-end to nerve-end. I used to think that it would be awful to hear the crowd at the next green screaming at somebody else's wonderful shot.

Some actors I've known have said that live, nationally televised drama was like that. In the theatre, I have seen three highly trained, respected actors all drop their lines at the same time. You assume when you're on stage that someone will substitute lines or even whisper when this happens, but to have all three lose their lines at the same moment is as horrifying as it is unheard of. Most actors can deal with the unexpected: a cat-call from the audience, a natural disaster, but the simple things like forgetting a line you've been speaking for weeks are the lapses that humble us.

Perhaps it's an oversimplification, but what I tell students with exam jitters is exactly what I tell actors who are nervous. Overprepare. Place yourself in the situation that if you go blank, the first thing you think of is how dumb it is to go up after all that work. Anger at yourself and a desire to get on with what needs to be done are much more helpful than reviewing your life in a flash or checking your pulse to see if you are going mad or dying.

Of course there are behavioral tricks we can practice to prepare for such situations. Since performance is physically taxing, prepare accordingly. If you were to go backstage at most theatres just before a performance, you would find actors doing exercises. There are as many regimens as there are individuals, but the majority are stretching, flexing, and relaxing. By stretching I don't mean to imply that to do this properly you should become as limber as a gymnast or dancer, and by flexing I don't mean to imply body-building. "Warming up" might be the best description for what they are doing. A performer is consciously flexing and loosening the major muscle groups, stretching the body, and breathing in a controlled and rhythmic way at the same time. I particularly like to link breathing with the exercises, to breath out as you touch your toes, for example, and then slowly inhale as you stretch upwards.

For the performer, the most important muscle group is located in the abdomen. It is the center for you physically. It supports your voice, and even when you are relaxed it is engaged. It is interesting that the ancient Greeks believed our center of consciousness was in the torso. The brain was thought to be an organ for cooling the blood.

Before performing or lecturing, do five to ten minutes of stretching, tensing, and relaxing. Nothing violent. No hurdle stretches or any of the marvels of contortion and control one finds on the final pages of a progressive exercise book. What I am suggesting is a useful regimen to be used as part of your preparation for performing. Do these before your classes, once or more during the day. Do them devoutly so that any benefits are constant. They are designed to be done in your office or in a small space in a hallway. They will probably have some affect on your nervousness, and they will certainly work on muscular tension which could lead to sore necks and hoarseness after a stint of teaching. They will also provide a transition into your teaching mode.

When I am teaching acting, I always begin the class with exercises. In addition to all the obvious benefits, there is also the one of providing a transition. An acting class is a very different experience from what my students are doing during the rest of their normal day. Sitting in a lecture or even reporting in a seminar class are very different experiences from presenting a scene or improvising a character. It's also true for me. I frequently walk into classes after meetings. I am not in the proper mood to participate. I have to remember that actors spend long years learning how to play conflicting moods of a character or even different characters in the same play. Why should I expect to be able to do this on the spur of the moment?

SUGGESTED EXERCISES

Here are some of the exercises I use. Let's begin with one in which we bend down, touching our toes, then slowly raise up. As our hands pass each part of our bodies, tighten the muscles, until we are stretched as high as possible, completely tensed. This is done on an eight count. We hold for a moment and then collapse, slowly not quickly, and touch the toes again, repeating the exercise perhaps three times. It's important to remember while doing this exercise not to throw your body forward after being fully extended and tensed. Instead, collapse slowly. Suddenly dropping down to touch your toes can cause back injury. (See Exercise #1, on the next page)

The second exercise involves placing your hands on your hips and bend back until you see the ceiling, then pivot your upper body, looking up, from side to side at least twenty times. Don't worry about speed; this exercise lets you explore your back for kinks. (See Exercise #2)

The third exercise in this series of stretching, flexing, and relaxing exercises is one in which you take a stride forward with your right foot and keep the left foot in place with the heel planted. Stretch forward, locking your hands and turning them inside out. (See Exercise #3)

The last of these exercises is the popular "isolations." Stand straight, tuck your chin to your chest twice to stretch the muscles in the back of your neck, and then rotate your head from left to right four times and from right to left four times. Leave the rest of your body immobile. This shouldn't be a completely relaxed movement, but it should be done with some "power" and control. After you've rotated your head, do your shoulders, full torso, hips, and then knees. Take your time. Explore each area of your body, but don't use undo force or speed and make the circles described by each part of your body as wide as possible. (See Exercise #4)

After these "warm-up" exercises, we work with the voice and breathing. When this is introduced in the workshop, I explain that one problem people have with projecting the voice is that they misunderstand the mechanics for producing sound. They believe

60

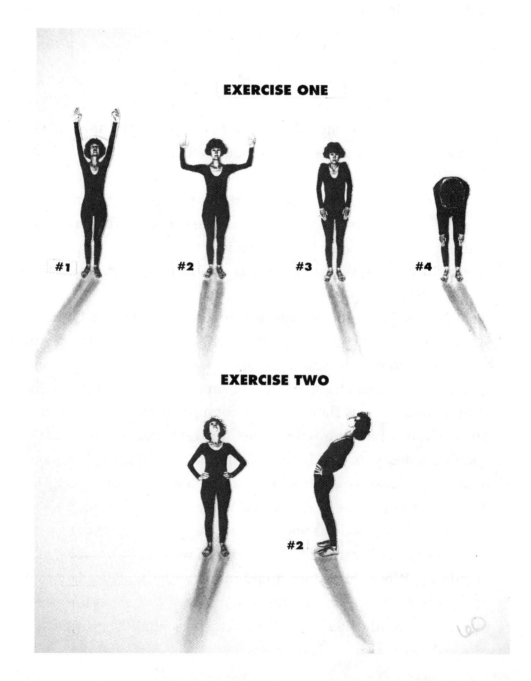

EXERCISE ONE

#1 #2 #3 #4

EXERCISE TWO

#2

EXERCISE THREE

#1   #2

EXERCISE FOUR

#2   #3   #4

that taking a deep breath is a matter of raising and expanding the chest, and that sound is somehow connected with a tightening of the throat. Doesn't volume come from squeezing the vocal chords? Not only is this wrong, it's painful. The vocal chords are vibrated by a column of air pushed from the lungs by the diaphragm, a muscle layer attached to the lungs which controls breathing. Your vocal chords are like the reed in a clarinet or the strings on a cello. Psychologically, however, the more you're convinced that sound begins and ends in the throat, the more problems you'll have. There is a myriad of muscle strands, bones, and cartilaginous structures for such activities as breathing and swallowing in this relatively small area. You may have heard it said that the human throat was never meant for speaking. The confusion and complexity of this part of our body explains such problems as hoarseness, unpleasant speaking voices, and dizziness. If you have improper support (breathing) and placement (the use of the resonating chambers in your face), lecturing can be agony. Incidentally, one of the marvels of the world can be a well-trained singer who sings beautifully despite what would for the rest of us be a silencing case of laryngitis.

The vocal chords are stroked by the column of air and our tongues and lips shape the sound into vowels. Then the lips and tongue interrupt the flow to form most of our consonants. Consonants are, in other words, interruptions of sound except for the so-called vibrants, like sounded "v" or "th." To understand what we're talking about, do the following exercise: (1) bend over slowly and touch your toes. Breath out as you do so, emptying your lungs of air. In this folded, bent-over position, open your mouth and let the air come in of its own accord. Feel what happens with your diaphragm. Now (2) stand with your back against a wall. Don't lose contact. Make a stomach, feel the air come in, and then press in the stomach muscles and feel the air pushed out. (3) Relax your jaw, expand your stomach, hold that breath for a moment, and then let it out and make a sound without any care about what the sound should be. Just make a sound. It is primal, perhaps, and it is also the basic building block of at least one famous school of vocal training, the Italian "bel canto" technique. It makes sense that with this one, basic vowel we can make all of the other vowel sounds just by shaping the lips and moving the tongue. Still using this "ahhh" sound, take a breath and push it with your stomach muscles. Do it rapidly. What are you doing? Something very familiar and primitive: laughing. All of us have laughed until our sides hurt. This is why.

The challenge now is to understand the interaction of stomach muscles, vocal chords, tongue, and lips. The basic concept is to keep a flow of air "supported" by the stomach muscles vibrating the chords and being articulated by the other structures, with interruptions for breaths coordinated with pauses and interruptions in speech. When we breathe, we actually expand our lung capacity by pulling down on the lungs which are being emptied. Find your own term for how it feels to take a breath properly. For me, the term "making a stomach" best describes it.

Now go on to scales using open vowels and "mmmmm". For example, "mah, mah, mah, mah, mah, mah, mah, mah" for each of the notes in a major scale. Stay in the middle of your range. Keep your jaw loose. I tell students to imagine that their jaws have been transformed into warm jello. Think of how a baby cries. Try that kind of breathing. I have known babies in my own household who could keep all of us awake for an entire night with their screams and have no sign of hoarseness in the morning. Sore stomach muscles, I suspect, but no other signs of damage.

Try singing a high note after loosening up with vocal exercises. Punch the note, supporting it with your stomach. Keep your jaw loose. If your voice breaks, sing a little lower or use more support. Make the sound fit your idea of singing that's lyrical and easy. Yell some phrases using your stomach. "Hello." "How are you?" Yelling isn't proper for a classroom presentation, but neither is a microphone. Good actors and good teachers should want to avoid barriers to communication, so avoid artificial effects. I realize that we are teaching a generation of young people who are used to overamplification and, in many instances, have already been damaged by it, but the ideal is still the use of the normal human voice in communication. In the theatre, I have observed actors who were "wired for sound" and whose softest whisper came through like a volcanic rumble. This struck me as mechanical and inhuman. I have attended lecture in which the teacher was coiled around a microphone as though it were a metal lollipop. What do actors do in a large or dead house? They may increase their volume, but they also articulate more carefully and put more resonance or "point" in their voices.

What do we mean by point? As you are making a sustained "aaah" sound, make a face, raising your whole facial mask, showing your upper teeth, and raising your eyebrows. Better yet, do this in a shower or cup your hand to your ear like an old-time radio announcer. Hear it? This is one of the oldest tricks in the book for increasing your audibility. You're not singing through your nose, as the saying goes, but actually singing against it, vibrating your facial mask. Even when the throat is tired or you have a cold, this is a fine way to adjust, and it shouldn't hurt your throat if you've learned to breathe properly and you keep your jaw relaxed. My final advice, however, would be to find a good voice teacher and take a few lessons. Any teacher should learn how to sing. You can use it in class, it will charm your family, provide relaxation and pleasure during long car trips, and teach you how to talk. By the way, doctors will tell you that most tone-deaf people are simply children who grew up without a song.

BODY LANGUAGE AND GESTURE

This discussion of exercises for the body and voice and the notion of preparing for teaching in the way that actors prepare for performance, leads naturally to a consideration of the other physical aspects of performance. For example, there are the matters of body language and gesture. Often actors will speak of their bodies as their "instrument," meaning that one's physical equipment is the equivalent of a musician's instrument. Here again there is reference to that informing principle that we begin with the individual's abilities, not some idealized model to which we should conform. As you may have noted already, the base-line questions are such as this: can you expend the energy necessary for a heavy day of teaching? Can you project your voice when the situation demands it? To these we would now add: can you project your feelings and ideas through your body, facial expressions, and gestures?

There are theories of communication which have carefully laid out whole systems of language through gesture. The famous, or infamous, *Delsarte* idea of standardized gesture to express specific attitudes is now widely ridiculed, but it grows out of a perfectly natural human tendency . In critiquing sessions, I often hear students say "If only so-and-so would look more serious when they talk," or "Don't splay your hand when you gesture that way." The damage done by such criticism is that it encourages us to think of performance as a mosaic of traits to be learned and used. If you study traditional dramatic forms like Chinese Opera or Japanese Kabuki,you can see this approach taken to an extreme. I feel that actors may pare away or adapt what they are doing, during the process of rehearsal, but the key questions in critiquing an actor's performance should address the individual's intention, meaning, and feeling. The stress is on how you come across as an individual, not as a composite of traits. In the beginning you should learn what works for you. Granted, there are certain facts about universal body language which should be considered. We can all agree on such terms as "open" and "closed" body language, meaning those actions which indicate a person is shutting out the rest of us or, conversely, including us, but there are matters of timing, necessity and particularity involved in gesture. What are some basic facial and body expressions which we can all identify?

In acting class I will sometimes have the students stand in a circle, watching one another, and then pick students and ask them to walk inside the circle expressing without words a particular attitude to their classmates. For example, I might give a phrase for them to act out like "I can lick any guy here," "There's been a death in my family," or "I've never felt better." Dancers or students with some pantomime training may overdo this exercise the first time. The former because there are ways that modern dancers, for instance, have been trained to draw attention to their movement and the ideas they express. Pantomimists lean toward exaggeration and simplification. When I get these reactions, I might say, "Be yourself. Walk it again. Think the feelings you have and let your body take care of itself." The result of this encouragement is a wide range of walks and attitudes, but with some surprising similarities. For one, there do seem to be two principal attitudes in human behavior: aggressiveness and fear. Like so many creatures, we show the first by puffing up, standing tall, swaggering, and smoothing out our movements. It's the dancer's term "expansion" or "opening." On the other hand, when we feel fear, humiliation, or depression, we become "closed." We are too hesitant or quick in our movements. We avoid contact with other people, walk with eyes downcast, and move around obstacles.

This much does seem to be a legitimate, shared physical language, but the ideas are so broad and the personal variations so endless that it communicates only in the most general way. Our suggestion would be that in matters of body language, you should think of the feeling, relate it to your own experience, and then allow your body to express it normally. Begin with this, not the stylized expression which you think everyone will know. In our everyday contact with one another, we come to understand one another's gestural language. For an actor, you begin by learning what is natural for yourself, and this helps you to better understand how another "individual" might express himself.

How does an actor make a character expressive and understandable? First, by being consistent. Secondly, by paring away what isn't necessary to the portrayal. And finally, by filling the role with emotion. In that great series of movie comedies that Alec Guinness did in the '50s which culminated with *The Lavender Hill Mob,* one of the great joys was watching Guinness lay out the physical language of his character. This always seemed to happen in the first few scenes. He would then orchestrate these actions during the rest of each film. These films were comedies and the actor could stylize the behaviors, but the characters were all different and original.

We are familiar with the trademark behavior of a Katharine Hepburn, James Cagney, or Spencer Tracy. There is much more to it than the way they move their bodies and speak. A number of more recent actors are much less easily pinned down (or imitated); Paul Newman, Dustin Hoffman, and Julie Harris come closer to the ideal of actors who fit themselves to a part. This is not meant as criticism of Spencer Tracy, for example, who was a fine actor both in the movies and on Broadway. However, I feel he was victim of the realities of movie financing. He was asked to do what had already proven successful at the box-office, so we saw the same character again and again. However, acting was not taken lightly by Tracy, even though he is frequently quoted as having said that "acting" was something you never wanted to be caught doing. What he meant was that your technique shouldn't show. He worked hard to make it appear effortless and was a stickler for attending to all of the controllable details of preparation, such as knowing one's lines and how to handle props.

The skillful actor will use a form of the same exercise I described at the beginning of this section. He is walking in a ring of people, expressing his emotion with his body and movement. Emotion and the actor's specific identification with it in a given situation is at the heart of the internal or "method" approach to acting. Auto-suggestion may be used, as well. If we open ourselves, slow the walk to a confident stride, smile, put our head up as we walk into a classroom, we convince not only our students but ourselves that it is a fine day and we are about to share it with them. One of the great truths of auto-suggestion is that there is a relationship between our bodies and minds.

Spencer Tracy

Bergson's theory of comedy says that what is funny is most often seemingly involuntary: the encrustation of the mechanical upon the human. This should conjure up any number of famous vaudeville or nightclub acts. I remember my father telling me about a vaudevillian who came on stage dressed as a professor, in robe and mortarboard. His only property was a hot-water radiator, which in this case had a mind of its own and was out to spoil his delivery by belching and banging at the wrong moments. How many comedy teams have worked with the premise of a very smart man attempting to dominate a slow one?

Jimmy Cagney

The laughs, whether it's the Smothers Brothers or Abbott and Costello, are based on the slower man's ability, often by chance, to get the best of his partner. But the audience has to understand the premise in order to enjoy it.

Once I was sitting in my high school's faculty lounge between classes when a pleasant, earnest colleague burst into the room. He seemed on the verge of tears, so the rest of us greeted him and then left him in peace. But later that day, a student from his eleven o'clock class told me what had happened.

It was an advanced chemistry class, and some of the brightest senior students were enrolled. They were definitely high-spirited. Early in the semester, I was told, they had realized that my friend had a mannerism. We all do. His was an unconscious catch-phrase: "Don'tcha know?" They started a pool. The rules were that everyone had to pay into the pot every class day and that the student who picked the exact number used during that class would receive the whole amount. Otherwise the money would be carried over. The contest had been going on for a week or more and the pool was now substantial. Think of the irony of the situation. It was a perfect example of the "encrustation of the mechanical upon the human" of Mr. Bergson's theory. That day a student hit the number. The tension really began to grow as the class ended. The rule was that the count went from the beginning of the class until the end. It was not bell to bell. This day the bell rang, the students started out, and then my friend, the teacher, held them back for a moment to give one last assignment. He noted, perhaps, the tension in the group standing closest to his desk. Who knows, but he felt called upon to explain that this was an important exercise which would help them on their next test, "Don'tcha know?" At this, the young man who had won the prize howled, "Ah, _ _ _ _!" The class fled to the hallway, and Loren lurched into the faculty lounge, eyes brimming.

We have all known this feeling. There has been a particular class which tended to laugh at the wrong moments, to share something among themselves which had nothing to do with the magic we were attempting to weave, or the good nature we wanted to share. Not infrequently it will be inadvertant humor caused by a mannerism. Probably this possibility is reason enough for ongoing arrangements with other teachers for occasional class visitations and the creation of opportunities for team teaching. You could also pick up clues from a televised taping of one of your sessions. I remember a television interview I did which I saw several months later. I watched with some interest and then began counting the number of times I touched my nose. I began to wonder if I had developed a new compulsion, and then I recalled that the week of the taping I had been plagued by hay fever. I wasn't going mad. My nose itched.

Gesture is natural to some people and not to others. An almost universal feeling that beginning teachers have is the strangeness of their arms hanging lifeless from their torsos and their hands, huge and useless, hanging from these. Young actors have the same complaint, unless they are given a gesture, which they will then overdo. It was intriguing to watch the British actor who played the clerk Newman Knox in the televised version of *Nicholas Nickleby* . His character had a wonderful knuckle-cracking gesture which drew your attention and spoke volumes about the relationship of this man's body to his emotions. But then, just when you wanted to make certain that everyone in the viewing room had noticed the mannerism, the actor saw to it that this gesture disappeared and was replaced by other more subtle indications of character. The role changed from cartoonishness to truth.

Gesture is yet another part of that physical presence of a teacher or actor which reinforces the meaning and feelings of the person or character. It is possible for someone to use a great deal of gesture effectively. It must be consistent and natural, but I'm sure that we have all known someone who did this. Most of us, however, have to decide how much to use. The rule of thumb should be, when in doubt, don't. Store up the energy for a gesture and then make it count.

I know we are all tired of the artificiality and redundancy of the "three good reasons" type of finger gesture which employs them to tick off each reason. A favorite elementary school joke was a make-believe routine between Roy Rogers and his Wonder Horse, Trigger. "All right, Trigger," Roy would say. "What's two and two." Then someone would stamp a foot heavily four times. "Just one more, Trigger," Roy would call out. "Just one more."

FACIAL EXPRESSIONS

There are certain facial expressions which we universally associate with specific feelings. Audiences watch our faces more closely than anything else. At a college graduation, I heard a graduating senior, who had the task of delivering the comic oration for his class, introduce Walter Cronkite. He commented that until today he had never seen the avuncular newscaster's legs, but he was pleased to report, as all could see, that Cronkite did have legs "and cute ones at that." Generations of Empire Englishmen learned how not to make the face the mirror of the soul; the same stoniness and lack of affect is a cliché with bankers, athletes, and cowboys in our own culture. One wonders why? Because it's dangerous. We might inadvertantly show what we really felt. The bland expression is a part of a sub-text of calm covering confusion which is used consciously or unconsciously, even by teachers. I think that among younger students there is a definite preference for teachers who express their feelings with their faces. Perhaps it is because they seem more open and this affect reads as friendliness.

ENERGY AND PACE

There are two terms used by theatre people which are frequently misunderstood: ENERGY and PACE. This confusion seems to me to grow out of people's awareness that time flies, as they say, when they are caught up in a performance. This leads even some critics to believe that ENERGY might exist separately from a performance and the fascination we have with a character and that PACE simply means to do a show or scene more rapidly. We cannot accomplish either unless the audience finds the material interesting and the performances engrossing. But PACE does seem to have the same quality as ENERGY in a given actor's work. In a way it could be considered to be the same thing as concentration or focus. Focus has already been suggested as part of the process of simplification and reduction of elements in a production, and the desire in the swift business of theatre to do less rather than more. But it is also a shrewd concentration by director and actor on

74

what's going on, a sense of how to direct the attention to the parts
and then to the whole. It is not SPEED. Often it just seems that
way.

The demand for energy, pace, and the underlying focus are in
large part what is really exhausting about performance, in a
classroom or on a stage. There is nothing easy about it. You feel
tension and anxiety beforehand, and during the performance you
are concentrating on verbalizing, physicalizing, and emotionalizing
the material, using your critical faculties to check your audience's
responses, and making subtle but split-second adjustments to the
conduct of the moment.

KING'S ENGLISH AND OVERHEAD PROJECTORS

There are two other matters which should be mentioned in
this discussion: the use of standard English (or American) and
some specific problems which teachers may have with certain
types of lectures and teaching aids.

As teachers, I believe most of us strive for an accent and usage
which will make us understandable to our students. Our
individuality may suffer, however, and some of us may refuse to
adjust. I love the story of the actor, Martin Gabel. If you don't recall
him, he was Arlene Francis' husband, an Ohioan who had long
since lost his regional accent as he became an actor and celebrity.
He had a special resonance and accent which could be called
Theatrical-Overblown. He was with two friends at a restaurant,
and two elderly ladies sitting nearby had been listening enraptured
as Gabel talked. When they got up to go, one stopped at his table.
"Excuse me, sir, but my friend and I are enchanted with your

accent. What is it?" Gabel smiled, "Affected, madame, affected."

Many American actors have had obvious regional accents. Henry Fonda's was a famous one. We loved him for it, but he never played Macbeth. George C. Scott and Paul Newman are both Mid-Westerners. They can play anything they want. Have you ever hear the mannered tones of F.D.R. or the nasal twang of Truman? Of course you know the standard sounds of Reagan. Pick your poison, but realize that it's an important part of what you do and how you initially come across. One of the great American put-ons is the highly educated economist from Harvard, who pretends to be a hayseed from Des Moines. I've met him. Perhaps you have too. It can be a perfect example of sub-text and misdirection.

Speaking of put-ons, let's mention add-ons, like those slide projectors, overheads, and assorted gadgets which we are tempted to use in class. I have never minded blackboard work so long as the teacher doesn't use it as a way to avoid engaging the class. Perhaps overhead projectors can be used while the teacher talks and the students watch and listen. I would start with minimal information on the transparency and then add more with a grease pen while I talk. I want the lecturer, not the devices he uses. Even those who have a fine hand for lettering and drawing should remember what "upstaging" means in the theatre. It can happen anywhere and be done by anything, including small animals, attractive children, and machinery.

People, I'm convinced, learn best from people. The survival of theatre in this age of movies, television, and now holographs attests to the power of "live" performance. What the students need to have in front of them is that most complex of all communicators, a moving, twitching, smiling, reacting teacher. The essential problem in education must still be how to reduce the length of the log the teacher and the student are sitting on rather than trying to find less human ways to teach.

CHAPTER 4
HONESTY

CHAPTER 4: HONESTY

Imagine having to persuade someone of the truth of what you're saying. It can be a small or monumental fact, but you must persuade them. How would you go about doing this? Now imagine having the same task with a group of twelve students, a typical seminar class. What new problems do you have? When you were dealing with one listener, you probably used eye-contact, physical closeness, and an intimate tone of voice, but now there are more of them and a table separating you. Now imagine standing in front of a class of forty. Can you project honesty in these three situations? I am reminded of a facetious newsletter I saw once. It had a list of truly difficult doctoral examinations. The one in Speech Communications was a lulu. You were to face a maddened mob and persuade them to act rationally in an address delivered in an ancient tongue other than Latin or Greek. We've all had days like that.

The point is that using honesty as a conscious tool in teaching is something that we either feel is beyond our grasp or to be used only in very special situations. It might be reassuring to know that it is also extremely elusive for beginning actors. Learning how to project honesty, by the way, is the subject of early lessons in internal acting. Honesty is considered the base-line for all the techniques an actor uses, as well as being demanded in almost all scripts. After all, in the great dramas of our culture there are almost as many roles for naive Ophelia as there are for cunning Claudius, and as many honest Othellos as there are deceitful Iagos. At such training schools as the Neighborhood Playhouse in New York City, honesty is the focus of much of the first year's training.

*(Opposite) Dr. William J. Griswold, Professor of History, Colorado State University. (Photo: The C.S.U. **Collegian**)*

Actually, despite what you might think, it is very hard to project this emotion. In the abstract, most of us can imagine communicating the truth even when we may disagree with a character we are portraying, but when it has to go beyond the first row of a theatre the problems multiply.

Granted there are people whose "honest faces" or "earnestness" or reputation seem to predispose an audience to believe them. People assume that such credibility is a gift and not the result of hard work and practice. You might think of ministers and politicians you've met and heard who didn't have the gift and who dearly needed it. What most teachers do when they cannot project honesty is to adopt neutrality. When I look back at my own student days, I'm amazed at how many intelligent, kind, reputable professors and teachers I had who were guilty of underplaying their interest in their subject, of burying themselves in notes when lecturing, and of ignoring even the students in the front row of their classrooms. Several of these men in my own experience were charming and helpful in an office visit, one on one, or wrote beautifully, or inadvertantly projected a kind of vulnerability which made us apologize for their short-comings. What agony it must be to be forced to speak and perform when you have no stomach for it. I wonder if an understanding of how to project honesty would have helped them?

The sorts of statements we are concerned with here are ones which involve values and feelings. We are not speaking of "honesty" in remarks on the weather, trivia, or the language of social interaction. There are many kinds of statements which a teacher might make, using honesty. Let's imagine that it's the first day of class. The teacher wants to make it clear that:

"I want all of you to do well in this class."

"I am available for conferences. If we miss connections, try again. I want to see you."

"The examinations will be biased in favor of your improvement."

"Women have as much right to careers in this field as men."

You can think of examples which have more to do with your situation, feelings about your students, and subject matter. But these are meant as examples of the sorts of ideas a teacher will express if interested in connecting significantly with their students. Given the willingness, the next problem is how one projects such ideas honestly. We are talking about everyone, not just those individuals who hug everyone and exude natural warmth. These are individual matters. As I have already said, I want people to be themselves, but to communicate more effectively. We are asking what acting can tell us that will help in this process. There are examples to be taken from the theatre, where it is not at all unusual for two actors to be radically different in their approach to a character and yet both be considered excellent in their protrayals.

Paul Scofield is a seemingly dry, deliberate, and restrained actor who has had considerable success in a variety of roles. Morris Carnovsky, on the other hand, is an equally famous actor who projects warmth and physicality. Both have become associated with the role of Lear in Shakespeare's *King Lear* and are equally famous for it. And it is not just a matter of one's taste. Both men's portrayals have a range, logic, and depth of emotion which give them similar validity and power.

In doing research for this study, I reread one of the most popular stories in English about teachers and teaching. It was *Goodbye, Mister Chips*, by James Hilton. I must have been influenced by the sentimental movie starring Robert Donat, because I was surprised at the novel's very honest portrayal of a man who had failed at his first teaching post because he was a poor disciplinarian. Later he succeeded by balancing kindliness with irony. He survived but it left him marked by a number of personal idiosyncrasies which would have sunk a lesser personality. This famous appreciation of teachers is, actually, a fairly credible description of one man's discovery of how to be effective despite shortcomings.

Some teachers will establish their particular relationship with a class early in the semester, while others will take longer. Again, it is comparable to a

Morris
Carnovsky

theatrical situation. There are many roles which require the actress or actor to sustain and wait for the character to be established. Two famous examples are Mother Courage in Brecht's *Mother Courage and Her Children* and Eliza Gant in Thomas Wolfe's *Look Homeward, Angel*, as adapted by Ketti Fring. In both instances the dramas would be marred if the actors were allowed to make their characters immediately likable or in some other way to soften aspects of the characters as the plays progress. The end result of the intended progression is that we come to sympathize with both women and to admire them in a very special way.

No matter which extreme is tended toward, consistency is demanded of teachers, some clear evidence of the connection between what we are saying and what we seem to intend it to mean, day after day. This should not, however, be a radical change from how we would normally express it in our private lives. It is rather an amplification and focussing of it for a group of students. Another example of an effective teacher comes to mind. Dr. Prager was a famous engineer who taught at Brown University in Rhode Island for many years. His colleagues held him in awe, because he was so well organized, incisive, and brilliant. However, the stereotype of a German professor didn't fit. "Prager also brought this organization into the classroom," a colleague wrote. "Anything he did he did thoroughly . . . Prager was especially gifted in interpreting the work in his specialty in such a way that people in other fields could easily understand it. When he presented material, it was always clear. The message never got lost . . ." Was this the strength of his teaching, as well? Yes, but he also had another attribute. As he himself said of his favorite type of student, "I especially like working with fresh minds, not with a mentality that has already acquired prejudices. . . . But freshmen, ah, they are a pleasure to teach."[1] He meant it, and the proof was that it was never necessary for one to get an appointment with the world-renowned Doctor Professor Prager. They were free to come in at any time for help and advice. He was a fine teacher.

PROJECTING HONESTY

How can a person learn to project honesty? There are two important concepts to bear in mind when borrowing the techniques used in actor training. The first of these is the concept of the necessity for the interaction of actor and audience in the creation of the effect. It cannot happen in a vacuum. Trained actors can recreate it from recollection, but beginners must experience it many times, so in an acting class it is essential to have the other students tell you how you come across again and again. The other concept is that of learning how to monitor your own performance: to see your audience's reaction and adjust to it moment to moment. Let's deal with the first.

Robert Frost, the American poet, wrote a poem which I frequently quote when I'm teaching beginners how to be honest in performance. Its name is *The Silken Tent,* and many critics believe it was written about his wife, a woman he describes metaphorically as being like a silken tent, "loosely bound / By countless silken ties of love and thought / To everything on earth the compass round . . ." The tent is balanced and full, and when the wind blows some of the restraining cables are made taut and others loosen, but the tent still keeps its shape. The tent's pole, the woman's soul in this reading, wavers or swings in a wind, but always points upward. The tent goes this way or that, tightening the ties or answering the tugs of this or that demand, but never loses its orientation or identity.

A wonderful thing about the poem is that it is much like what it describes. It is one sentence of fourteen lines, each line a guy holding down the tent which it is describing. I point this out and then I note the two salient features of the work which should be very important to them. The first is the idea of contrary forces giving form and life to something inanimate. The obvious connection I make is to actors and audience interacting to bring life to a play script, or actors playing against one another to vitalize a scene for an audience. The other feature of the poem I point out to them is the way that the object itself, the dead words on the page, already have a resemblance to the dynamic of the object they are suggesting. It may not "look" like a tent, but its lines behave like the guys it describes. It stretches and pulls and finally inflates and stands erect. And talking of this poem in this way always reminds me to recite to them the last lines of yet another poem, W. B. Yeats' *Among School Children*, which ends with the lines:

> O chestnut-tree, great-rooted blossomer,
> Are you the leaf, the blossom or the bole?
> O body swayed to music, O brightening glance,
> How can we know the dancer from the dance?

Does this creation of art and reality end with poetry and drama? Of course not. Think of dissonance and harmony in music, angularity and repose in sculpture, and agreement and challenge in a speech. Conflict and repose are the essence of theatre, and are obviously the dynamics from which all powerful communication comes. One of the lessons I want to teach is how to avoid neutralizing this dynamic, sublimating the tension, letting the tent collapse, if you will. The stage actor has an advantage over a teacher in that there are usually other actors on stage. As Charles McGraw says in *Acting is Believing,* "Another way in which the actor directs his attention is toward other actors. He attempts to influence the people with whom he is playing. He yields to or resists their influence in turn. The 'connection' established by this process is one of the actor's surest sources of stimulation and one of the most rewarding theatre experiences for the audience."[2]

Performance is special and so it deserves preparation. What could a teacher use as a substitute for another actor? A time-honored technique would be rehearsing your lecture with someone listening. Part of what informs the rehearsing of actors is the imperative that when they go into production, every show should be of the same quality. Part of the pride an actor has in her craft is expressed in the ability to give eight good performances a week. This is much more than a response to the notion that "the play must go on." Rather, the rule is that the play "will" go on and small audience or overflowing, they will be given the same quality of performance.

A common failing of young actors is that they are energized by large and enthusiastic audiences, while they are depressed by small ones, no matter how enthusiastic. Experienced, professional actors learn to cope with this and other problems of the career. By and large they have amazing resiliency and energy. It goes with the territory. Self-respecting teachers should build the same expectations for themselves. Performance cannot be an on-again, off-again proposition. And if we expect it of ourselves, we will certainly expect it of our students. I remember a teacher friend who grew weary of a college student who was frequently absent and finally pulled him aside and asked, "If you bought groceries at the super market, would you leave them on the counter after paying for them?"

The other important concept in learning to project honesty is the concept of becoming your own critic. In the opening chapter, I discussed the need to develop split-focus: the ability to monitor how you're coming across even as you make your presentation. I should say more about this here. The feeling I have when I am using split-focus in a lecture is like blinking. One moment I'm deeply involved in what I'm expressing and the next I'm removed and objective about how I'm coming across. It is never simultaneous. I know that I am unconsciouly watching for certain signs and also keeping a clock going in my head. The signs I watch for would be my personal interpretations of student attentiveness or receptivity or the lack of same. I say "personal" because I believe these signals are part of a backlog of experience each of us has had with audiences and how we come across. Of course there are general observations which we all make. In theatre we speak of "stilling" a house, a wonderful way to describe the attentiveness of an audience which is deeply involved in what is occurring on stage. By the same token, coughing and rustling are signs of lack of involvement. I find that both of these measurements are at work in class. A third sign for me is the degree to which an individual student will look back at me and give some sign of agreement or interaction when I stop swinging my eyes across the class and fix my look on one person. Note-taking, by the way, may or may not be a sign of attentiveness. As a teacher I personally have a problem getting students to take down salient points. I realize that part of the cause of this is that I want them to be involved on a personal level in what we are discussing. A discursive, interactive style poses problems for note-taking. One solution is to hand out outlines or to put major points on the board before class or suggest that they get them in their notebooks during the class discussion. Another method I use is the assignment of one-page summaries which they hand in during the next class meeting.

Aggressiveness, cantankerousness, and impatience on the part of students is to be preferred to their boredom, inattention, or mopiness. Not everyone will agree with me in this, but I believe that education should be challenging for students and teachers. The real enemy for both is wasting time.

One of the best training grounds for teaching is public school. When I taught in high school, I had five or six classes a day and as many as three preparations. Having multiple sections of the same course also posed problems. You had to learn how to vary your signal, create new materials, and meet the needs of each group. During those years, I was particularly fond of teaching sophomores. My father always told me that at that age I was "halfway up fool's hill." He was right, but it's an exciting climb and it's enjoyable watching each new generation making it. My sophomores were alternately mature and childish, enthusiastic and "cool." I remember that I had two sophomore classes back to back one year. We were studying Dickens' *A Tale of Two Cities* and it was time to review the material prior to an exam. In the last minutes of the class I asked Irene Asendorf, a lovely, lanky young lady, to name the spies. "Roger Cly," she said, "and-and . . ." She hesitated. "Go on, Irene. Who's another?" She blushed and finally said, "John Bastard." The class roared, and I tried to yell over them and correct it to "Barsad," but the bell rang. All at the same time. Then the next class came in and Whitey, you can imagine him, tall, very blond, and goofy, was still laughing when the next bell rang. He'd obviously heard the story about Irene's answer, out in the hall. Finally, I challenged him. "All right, Whitey. You're laughing at what Irene said." "Yeah," he said with a smirk. "Well, Whitey, it's a perfectly good word." "Sure," he replied and the class laughed. "Do you know what it means?" "Sure," he answered. "What does it mean, Whitey?" "Well," he said, "it's a female dog." Bless sophomores.

There was a very good teacher whose final words before leaving the lunch room each day to meet a particularly lack-luster class were variations on "If you can't teach them, water them." He would get it out of his system. It is my contention, formed during those early years in a high school, that a sense of humor, enjoyment of students, and love of your subject will ultimately lead to effective teaching. This, plus the ability to criticize yourself and find ways to be effective without abandoning who you are. It is often very challenging and humbling. It is possible even with a class you've been teaching successfully for a year that one day nothing will work. Your humor or your attempts at persuading them through honesty fall flat. You always have to be prepared to examine your approach. One of my most embarrassing and, ultimately, most meaningful experiences in a high school classroom came about in just this way. I was in the final weeks of spring semester with a senior class in World Literature, a subject for non-college bound students. The district actually referred to it as "terminal" English. My reaction was to try to make it the best course they would have in high school. Its scope gave us the opportunity to read the best and most entertaining literature from all cultures. It had been a pleasant year with this particular class. I had been saving some of my favorite writers for the last week, among them Bobby Burns. I had introduced the poet the day before, saying to the class that they should come to class prepared to cry. I was going to move them deeply with the works of one of the funniest, saddest, and most unfortunate poets in our language.

That next day I gave them details of Burns' life and then began reading the more familiar poems in our text. I struggled to be eloquent and touching and repeatedly chided them for their failure to be sufficiently moved. The last poem I read, *The Banks o' Doon*, ends with the famous lines, "But my fause luver staw my rose, And left the thorn wi' me." I was genuinely touched by the poem and the situation it describes, and then I saw that at least one of the students had finally let go and was crying in the back row. The class ended and I sat down at my desk to do some work before my next class. I thought I was alone, but there beside my desk was a friend of the girl who had been so touched. "You're a jerk," she said. "You knew she was pregnant, didn't you." It was my turn to pay dues.

EMOTIONAL RECALL AND THE MAGIC IF

The specific techniques for learning how to project honesty are "Emotional Recall" and the "Magic If." All actors use yet another approach which we might call simplification. By it I mean the process of reducing materials to their basic parts, discovering their progression, and then learning these features of a work. Fuzzy thinking is a danger in all fields. I am reluctant to turn a group of actors loose on a play, to start the process of character building, before they have read it carefully as a document that demands analysis. I would feel the same uneasiness asking undergraduates in economics for the reasons behind the current recession as I would asking a group of actors for the meaning of Beckett's *Endgame* .

After preparing the role, I hope actors are able to grasp all aspects of the work. Before a performance we may talk about the meaning of the play and then visual the experience of the performance we are about to give, in much the same way that sports psychologists will take a skier or a gymnast through the event they are about to perform. Focus is as necessary as the underlying technique of blending meaning and feeling. It is the way to find clarity and energy in the performance. As for a teacher's use of these tools, there is no doubt in my mind that a clear understanding of the essential meaning of the materials to be taught is as important as previewing the actual performance. I still remember a final lecture given in graduate school by a seemingly predictable professor. What he did was to unexpectedly tie everything together for the entire year at the lecture's end. His usually dry delivery became vibrant and he smiled as he announced that he had just completed one of his famous circles. We had arrived at the point at which we had begun, and it was true, made remarkable sense, and we shared his unexpected excitement and broke into spontaneous applause.

Imagination, "Emotional Recall," and the "Magic If" are related. They are all means for creating an event before it has happened, to practice what we've never performed before, or to call back our feelings and experiences as a way of fleshing out what we are about to do. An actor uses all of them. When you are faced with developing a new character, you draw upon your own experiences that are similar to your character's; you imagine events and feelings you've never had, or heighten and focus upon underlying feelings. Stanislavski insisted that actors should leave their last character behind and go to the next with a clean slate.

What does all of this have to do with teaching and projecting honesty? There are at least three benefits from using these techniques. The first is developing imagination. Another is experimentation and practice, and the third is the creation of choices. As for the last, very little of what an actor invents or discovers in himself is used in the final portrayal of a character. Instead, during the process of rehearsal much is attempted, reacted to, and then discarded or reshaped. What is wanted is a rich, full flow of ideas which can then be subjected to interaction with other actors and the director as well as to one's own critical intelligence. Playwrights have their own equivalents for these acting techniques. Tennessee Williams, for example, often used his mornings to write brief, vivid scenes, unrelated to any other project, almost as though he were tapping his subconscious. When he wrote a play, it was often a process of reshaping, plotting, and patching together these vivid fragments. The great Henrik Ibsen, on the other hand, used another technique to prevent his critical faculty from blocking the creative. He wrote voluminous biographies of his characters, so that he would know how they might behave in unforeseen circumstances, then he would start writing the play in which they were to appear by writing the climax first and then moving backwards to the beginning.

Michael Chekhov, a student of Stanislavski and a great acting teacher in his own right, used the term Visualization for part of this technique, and stated, "If I feel it, I will show it." We can see how this fits into Stanislavski's overall perception of how the technique works. He called the "if" a lever which serves to "lift us out of everyday life onto the plane of imagination." A whole series of "if's" for which we invent answers create a character's circumstances. "The aim of the actor should be to use his technique to turn the play into a theatrical reality. In the process, imagination plays by far the greatest part."[3]

In Selden's *First Steps in Acting* , he describes imagery as "responsive movement and speech" which comes out of a keen awareness of the messages of our senses and feelings. As for the concept of emotional recall or memory, one of the many who have identified it and described how it works is Stanley Glenn. In his *The Complete Actor*, he points out that the playwright prescribes the action. One might ask how an actor's own experiences and feelings could fit into another's constructed reality. "There are many actors who make the mistake of substituting their own exact responses for those of the character," he writes, "just as there are those who believe that they must go out and undergo the exact experience of their character." These are not necessary or the point of the exercise. "The essential value of emotional memory is that it may enable the actor to better understand and believe in the emotional situation of the character, and that it will aid him in finding a way of executing the action demanded by the script without resorting to vague, generalized, and cliche-ridden responses."[4]

How can we use acting techniques to project honesty in a classroom? Let's begin by describing a "role" you might want to play: that of a caring, concerned teacher. The teacher is a person who sees students receiving great benefit from her classes. She is well organized, certainly, but also fair, comfortable with people, enthusiastic and open. Pick your own adjectives. What negatives might you have in mind when you go into this classroom? There has been poor attendance and an apparent lack of interest on the part of the students who do appear. You have feelings of nervousness and inadequacy. You might also feel resentment and hostility toward them. Perhaps you've described them to colleagues. "A bunch of duds." "Losers." "Typical undergraduates." Now your immediate objective is to turn all of this around from this day forward to semester's end, using techniques which an actor would use in creating a new character or role.

First, deal with your nervousness about facing this class. Most of us develop elaborate strategies for minimizing the affect a poor class has on us. As already suggested, part of this may be common sense. How can we assume that they are as against us as we believe them to be? They barely know us. The closest we can come to this being personal is that we may remind them of someone they know a lot better than they know us. However, if you want to turn this situation around, you'll have to accept the fact that you are not succeeding. Be certain that you have your materials well in hand, exams graded, and loose administrative duties tied down, then start the imaging. Imagine a successful class session. In particular think of the feelings you have had in another class or some other people experience when you were exhilarated, enjoying yourself, and receiving positive reinforcement. Was there a time when a class you were teaching hired the balloon man or gave you a gift? A time when you surprised yourself with your own sense of humor and the responsiveness of the class? Be particular. Recreate these experiences in detail. Dramatize them. Place faces. Maybe look up old class rolls. And don't doubt that such exercises yield powerful results. Once you've worked on them, they are there whenever you need them. There's the story of the young woman who asked the actress Geraldine Fitzgerald how she managed to cry on demand. Ms. Fitzgerald was then and is now a marvellous technical actress who had solved this problem with care and practice. She had found some experience to use. The young actress must have thought it was a trick or short-cut, so she asked what it was. "None of your damn business," Fitzgerald answered. By the same token, the positive images you recreate will be no one else's "damn business." Use them exactly as some people use music or a walk before dinner. Let the experiences or image trigger the feeling. Fill your mind with it and allow your body to respond naturally.

If you cannot fill in the details or you've repressed the good experiences, imagine them happening, the "Magic If." Build bridges, as Hagen says, between what you have known and what you're trying to construct. Do you remember your first days in a classroom? Could you make connections between that experience and other times, perhaps when you were a student yourself? Can you visualize a particularly excellent teacher you studied after and recall how she came across, the feelings she brought out in you?

Now imagine what the class will be like tomorrow, when you

next meet with them. As you think over the major points to be made, create clusters of feeling and sensation. "When I say this, then I'll feel like this." Anticipate and rehearse. One of the great problems drama teachers have in high schools is getting the student actors to commit themselves to specific behaviors in rehearsal. Remember the tender boy girl scenes which they refused to do? Despite their promises to do it and do it well when they appeared before an audience, they actually panicked when their parents and friends were present. Clearly the embarrassment and difficulty in facing this challenge will not go away and must be handled beforehand if you have any hope of its coming out right.

As concerns the matter of honesty, you will have to monitor it during the lecture, but try to isolate the feelings you have when you're being honest. Find adjectives before, after, or during the experience. Describe the feeling so that you can use it again. There are obviously hundreds, but here are a few of the adjectives which might describe the focus you have during your class: you are concerned, affected, fascinated, engrossed, earnest, enthusiastic, intrigued, absorbed, excited, curious, intent, or fervent, inquisitive, nosey, keen, zealous, or avid. Pick your own term for the underlying focus of your lecture and stick to it. Let this and your feelings about the experience take care of the way you physicalize it. Again, the point is to deal with the larger moments and ideas and not to be overwhelmed by your own data or the countless impressions you may be receiving on how you're coming across.

There are other impressions that people have had of similar experiences which may help you before, during, and after it. There are many sports in which the key to success is not only practice but learning how to let yourself go. Skiing and golfing are two that immediately come to mind. If you tense before going down a slope or hesitate before you swing a club, your coordination seems to fall apart. In skiing everything begins to work for the beginner as you gain speed. Lecturing seems like this. As you gain momentum, the impressions you receive require immediate adjustments. There's no time for deliberation.

An analogy to playing comedy may help. One of the most difficult techniques to master is learning how to "time" laughs. Each audience will vary in its responses. Your intention is not to let the audience take over. You don't want them to feel that you need the laughs, but you also don't want to "kill" their enthusiasm by cutting them off. Frequently a good playwright will arrange the jokes so that there is a culminating "topper" which releases all the pent-up energy created by cutting them off on their responses to the earlier jokes. The adjustments actors are making in this instance are slight but to the point. If there are large adjustments to be made this will happen in a special rehearsal. The teacher learning how to project honesty has much greater latitude, but still must resist making large adjustments on what has been planned before.

A few more warnings. As the saying goes, you might as well be hanged for a wolf as a lamb. Or the one I love to use in theatre: if you are telling a lie in the theatre, tell a whopper. The point is, handle any performance as a larger than life opportunity. You can always cut back, but it's difficult to add on. I am still bemused by a speaker I saw who went one better than anything I'm promoting here. His speech began with fifteen minutes of non-stop magic, off-the-wall humor, horseplay, and audience participation. Gradually he began to insert serious comments and his intention came into focus: "Pay attention. We've had fun; now I have something important to say. " I have rarely felt so off-balance in an audience. It was exhilarating and commanding. I will never be able to pull it off myself, but, like they say, I've been to the mountain. In the next chapter we will describe a category of effects used by this speaker: sub-text.

As you practice honesty, don't rush to change your approach. As suggested, sometimes it takes longer for a particular teacher to establish herself with a class, just as there are characters in a play or movie that "grow on you."

I think it is very important to believe in what you are doing, but remain flexible and keep your priorities in order. If you don't like your material, the students or your teaching method, change some or all of them. I may envy another teacher's style or popularity, but in the final analysis they're hers, not mine. I have my role to play on my stage.

A final point, don't rest with honesty, when you've learned to project it. All art requires variety and contrast. Move along now to the possibilities of sub-text.

---

[1]Jay Barry, "Gentlemen Under the Elms" (Providence, Rhode Island: Brown University), p.91.

[2]Charles McGaw, "Acting Is Believing," 4th ed. (New York: Holt, Rinehart and Winston, Inc., 1980), p.59.

[3]Constantin Stanislavski, "An Actor Prepares," trans. Elizabeth Reynolds Hapgood (New York: Theatre Arts Books, 1936), p.15.

[4] Stanley L. Glenn, "The Complete Actor" (Boston: Allyn and Bacon, Inc., 1977), p.58.

CHAPTER 5
SUB-TEXT

CHAPTER 5: SUB-TEXT

It must be clear to everyone that there are many more words in everybody's vocabularies than could be looked up in a dictionary. Think of the many meanings which can be given to the word "really" by changing the inflection, or a phrase like "that's nice," or even to a non-verbal like silence. By the way, in theatre the word PAUSE in a script is often mightier than words. But as for our vocabulary, or that used by people speaking every known language, we have a great many ways to expand our meaning. I was told a story about a college logic teacher who informed his class that in language as in algebra, two negatives equalled a positive, but two positives are always a positive. He gave the example, "I don't not know." From the rear of the room a voice commented sarcastically, "Sure, sure."

We have many names for this use of expanded meaning. Sarcasm is one. Others are humor, wit, absurdity, arrogance, and silliness. The list goes on and on, but none of them works unless the listener or a third party knows that it is intended. Condescension, for example, may be natural for some people but not necessarily intentional. E.M. Forster's English colonials in *A Passage to India* were largely unaware of their attitude toward the Indians. The novelist makes the point that they should have been. I recall seeing the film made from this novel in a neighborhood theatre in London and being very aware of the audience's acute embarrassment. They understood Forster's sub-text much more acutely than any movie audience would in America.

Since this is a fact of our everyday communication, it should not be surprising that playwrights have used sub-text since the

(Opposite) **Mother Courage and Her Children** *by Bertolt Brecht. Grinnell College Theatre Production, directed by Porter Woods, 1969.*

beginnings of drama. Actually, the notion that theatre pretends to be life could be seen as the basic sub-text of the art form. Irony is the term we use for it. This word seems to have come from an early Greek root which suggests "crazy like a fox," an animal which the American poet Wendell Berry once described as making "more tracks than necessary, and some in the wrong direction." During the Hellenistic era, it was used as a noun to name those shrewd servants of dull masters who actually ran things in their households.

A larger form of verbalized sub-text has to do with the overall objective of a statement or piece of communication. Another name for this could be "intention." When we use honesty we might be speaking of our intention to show "anger" or "caring" and match it with our surface behavior. But in sub-text the meaning or objective is submerged, often contradictory to what is being said and done. For example, think of those comics whose careers are built on their ability to insult people in original and outrageous ways. Don Rickles comes to mind. During one of his frequent visits to the *Johnny Carson Show*, he commented that Ed McMahon, Johnny's side-kick, "makes more money sitting with his mouth shut than anyone in the world." Strange as it sounds Rickles meant this as a friendly insult. and both the victim and the audience understood this and laughed.

A third form of sub-text might be called dramatization. Almost all children pass through a stage when they invent imaginary playmates to excuse behavior or invent experiences they wish they'd seen or done. Lying and exaggeration are equally natural. Storytelling grew out of this human trait, and then theatre. To the literal minded, theatre may be thought of as an art which passes off falsehoods as truth. Think of the good storyteller who entertains all of us at a party. She invents characters, gives them voices, creates a narrative structure, and describes places and people. There are probably two intentions underlying this behavior: to entertain and to create the illusion of truth.

A fourth common form of sub-text is silence. In modern scripts one frequently sees this direction: PAUSE. Such modern playwrights as Beckett, Pinter, and Albee use it often. But I don't assume for a moment that this device is new. I believe that actors and playwrights have known about this for centuries, but it was a technique for delivering a line, not a written stage direction. Think of the wonderful moment in Shakespeare's *A Midsummer Night's Dream* when Bottom wakes up. We know he has been transformed into an ass. As he examines himself he does what we now call a "double-take." It takes place during his long pause between looking and understanding. The audience is made God at that moment, knowing something the character doesn't know and watching him learn it. As for the rest of us, we use silence as sub-text when we pretend not to hear something that we feel shouldn't have been said. We point our behavior so that it is clear to the other person what we mean to express. A friend, who worked in a school for the deaf, told of her frustration when she reprimanded young students only to have them close their eyes so they couldn't see her signing or talking.

Several of the preceding are non-verbal or physicalized sub-text. Perhaps the most clearly understood of this category are those facial expressions and gestures that a culture has conventionalized. Think of an Italian's shrug, a Frenchman's raised eyebrows, or the face made by a taxi-driver in any large city in the world when your tip is less than he expected. Most often, however, gesture and expression are used in connection with what is being said. They can be used as contrast or amplification but are a definite part of the sub-text. The same goes for a lack of expression when one is expected: the English gentleman's stiff upper lip in the face of adversity or the look from Clint Eastwood as Dirty Harry just before he says, "Make my day."

Another form of physicalized sub-text involves large body movements. As we have noted, all humans could be classified as belonging to one of two groups: those who fight or those who run. In dance and theatre much is made of "open" and "closed" postures and movements as signs of aggressiveness or shyness. This seems to be universal. Have you ever seen traditional Japanese couples meet in a public place? The women step back behind their husbands while the men indicate respect for one another's social position by bobbing lower and lower. In the emperor's court in China, as in the Pope's ordination of his cardinals in the Vatican, the ultimate sign of submission was and is to stretch prostrate on the floor before your ruler.

Much is written nowadays about self-imaging and body language. Even our current obsession with exercise and sports can be interpreted as a demonstartion of our belief that the way we feel about our bodies can affect the way other people react to us. Vitality, self-confidence, and energy are all projected by openness and forms of physical aggressiveness. As for sub-text, imagine a situation in which a superbly trim and fit younger man is standing tall as he tells an older, flabby, round-shouldered man, "You're right, sir. You're the better man."

As with other forms of sub-text, there is a use of the PAUSE in physical behavior. Two images come to mind. Do you remember how slowly Cleveland's Jim Brown would rise after a tackle and return to the huddle? Was he injured? Just getting back his strength? And Jim Thorpe, possibly the greatest athlete America has ever produced, would fall asleep on the bench while he was playing with the Carlisle Indians.

Most often when we are using sub-text in our communication, we combine the verbal and the physical. What if a person were handicapped? I vividly remember a successful teacher who was paralyzed and wheelchair bound. His use of his upper body was very limited, but he was capable of expressing a wide range of emotions with his hands, face, and voice. Pantomimists, traditionally voiceless, employ exaggeration, facial expression, and stylized movement as their means of conveying thought. If you ever saw the inspired silent movie skits of Imogene Coca and Sid Caesar on *The Show of Shows* or Red Skelton's nightclub performances and television show, you would know that there were no limits to the range of effects used by these great clowns, including sub-text. Film lovers know the work of Chaplin, Keaton, Laurel and Hardy, and the ascerbic W. C. Fields, whose billiard game with a twisted cue was one of the great pantomime performances. By the way, Fields was anything but kind to his competition. According to his friend Gene Fowler, the comic left a Chaplin movie, the first he'd ever seen, after only a few minutes and went to sit in Fowler's car. Fowler watched the movie and then rejoined Fields. How had he liked Chaplin's work? Fields replied, "Goddamn ballet dancer."

When big-time radio arrived, a number of early performers couldn't make the change, but others like Fred Allen, Jack Benny, and Groucho Marx were superbly versatile. Granted, they most often worked within a framework of situation comedy and continued to use the same characters they had developed in vaudeville and silent movies, but their skill with sub-text translated to the new media.

Think of these comics and then compare them to those people who fail to communicate even when they can combine both the physical and verbal in attempts at sub-text. How many embarrassingly poor comics have we seen in a lifetime? How many good stories have been ruined by a nervous or clumsy storyteller? How many fascinating characters have been over- or under-played by inadequate actors in movies, plays, and on television. Sub-text is a part of everyone's life, an expansion of what we say and understand which enriches our communication, but it demands practice.

TRAINING ACTORS IN SUB-TEXT

Honesty, as I've pointed out, is the baseline attitude for an actor. You have to learn how to project it to your audience, but having mastered this, actors must learn sub-text. It is a matter of saying one thing and meaning something else. In the theatre, as in everyday life, it must be projected to the audience though not always to the victim. In the theatre there are gradations. On stage, Iago is a character whose duplicity should be obvious to everyone except Othello. In the case of Hamlet, his sub-text might be hesitancy or doubt of the intentions of the ghost, or a psychological problem with his attachment to his mother. In *Hamlet* as in many modern plays, the underlying behavior must be there from the outset, so that by play's end the audience can think back and see the foundations for the later action. They can also be surprised by what happens and then ascertain the motivation from clues given and underlined, and ultimately make sense of a very complex character and play. Generally speaking, we expect key scenes to be consummately thought out and acted, but not overdone, so that the sub-texts are clear, but not exaggerated. In melodrama, the characters may provoke hisses and laughter and cheers, but in today's performances of great dramas, and certainly in modern realistic and naturalistic plays, economy of means and subtlety are prized.

The problems posed by the use of sub-text can be demonstrated by the story of the first performance of Anton Chekhov's *The Seagull,* at the Alexandrinsky Theatre in St. Petersburg in 1896. The company was used to French farces, and the night of the opening was also a benefit performance for a popular comic actress, so the audience was baffled by what was going on, and the production was a disaster. In short, the audience laughed when it should have winced, and they were embarrassed when they should have been touched. The essence of Chekhov as a playwright is his feeling for ordinary events and the complexity of human relationships. Directors and actors must understand his use of sub-text and communicate it to their audiences. Chekhov was so disheartened by this experience that he refused to allow another production. Two years later Stanislavski prevailed on him to allow the new Moscow Art Theatre to produce this play again. It was successful this time because, among other things, a new acting style had been developed by its director. The playing was much less obvious and theatrical, the characterizations were based on real people and their experiences and feelings, rather than on abstractions, and the audiences was given the opportunity to learn how to react to the material.

As already noted, sub-text depends on the audience's understanding of what isn't being said. Chekhov was already famous for his short stories and novellas in which his characters were often very ordinary people who were treated with compassion and wonderful detail. This had to be communicated as a new stagecraft. Furthermore, his plots might seem fragmentary and incomplete, but were not only reminiscent of the technique he used in his prose works, but also very close to the way most of us remember what we live through. He described life as a series of vivid or sometimes inconsequential moments, vaguely connected to one another, like photos in an album or our recollections of past experiences. Chekhov's plays, it turned out, pointed the way to a new form of expression in the theatre: Impressionism. A rival and contemporary trend was represented by Henrik Ibsen: Social Realism. Both were to bring sub-text acting to new levels of complexity and art, ushering in the popular theatre we have today.

SUB-TEXT FOR TEACHERS

So, how can teachers use sub-text? Most of us consider teaching a part of our everyday lives, not something removed. We don't change our basic orientation to the world or our fellow humans when we step into the classroom. Sub-text is very much a part of our everyday lives.

Another key reason for exploring its use in our teaching is the need that all of us have for variety in our communicating. Honesty needs contrast. Think of what life would be like without a sense of humor and how weary we all become when all of the answers we are given are "straight." How do we feel about people who always say exactly what they mean without a shred of humor?

Let's take a look at the most common form of sub-text, humor, and see how it might relate to teaching. It's surprising how little theorizing has been done about humor. It seems to be one of those subjects everyone knows about and uses, but few can describe. In theatre, for example, after we have discussed Bergson's theory of "the encrustation of the mechanical upon the natural" and Sigmund Freud's notion of humor being socially acceptable aggression, we are left with only descriptive studies. In the classroom, you will probably work with the two basic types: physical and verbal humor. Sub-division of the latter might be described as garden variety wit and wisecracking. By the way, don't all of us have a friend who is witty: the quiet

> *Wit is*
>
> *what*
>
> *you wish*
>
> *you'd said.*
>
> - Heywood Broun
>
> (*The Algonquin Wits*, p. 73)

> *Wit has truth in it; wisecracking is simply calisthentics with words.*
>
> - Dorothy Parker
>
> (**The Algonquin Wits, p. 124**)

voice in the corner who can hush a room when she finally speaks. But most of us have to plan comedy in advance. Think of the speeches you've heard which started with a joke you've already heard. It must be said that we appreciate the attempt, but I personally dread the remark that inevitably follows: "But now to be serious." When it comes to wit, I think of Winston Churchill. If you don't know any of the Lady Astor stories, one of the most famous was of an argument he and she had which ended when Lady Astor proclaimied that if she were married to Sir Winston, she would put posion in his orange juice. He immediately replied, "And if I were married to you, Lady Astor, I would drink it." My thought is that English public schools must have had a course in repartee or quick wittedness. My all-time favorite comeback is one I first heard attributed to William Pitt, an early champion of the Colonists prior to the American Revolution. He was debating in the House of Lords, when one of his opponents charged that Pitt would either die of French disease (syphillis) or on the gallows. Pitt immediately stood to reply. "T'is impossible, my lord," he shouted. "For I shall never embrace either your mistress or your politics." One can look long and hard for repartee like that in our own august chambers, where strong feelings in the early days, at least, were expressed with threats, canings, and gunshots.

I am not against teachers learning to feign spontaneity. Actors do it all the time with varying degrees of effectiveness, but then we know they're really not saying their own words. It would probably be better to counterfeit wittiness than to do what most of us do: stand with our mouths open waiting for the proper retort to come out. Don't you know the feeling? A Mack truck could drive through this opening. And then it's too late. You'll think of the answer when you get home. Planning ahead may be our only hope, or the appearance of wittiness in the absence of the same. Knowing looks or a wink may fool those around us.

I stood in a post office in northern Vermont one sweltering August afternoon. A farmer stood beside me at the package counter. Lying on the ledge in front of us was a small, carefully wrapped box with a brilliant red label. There was an address but the noticable part of the label were the words, in white block letters, BULL SEMEN. The farmer and I stood there, silent, as the seconds ticked by. It is my guess that he was doing what I was doing: furiously hunting for a witty comment. Vermont farmers are supposed to be famous for them. Then the postal clerk moved toward us and the moment passed. If it ever happened again, I . . . still don't have a good line.

I have been lucky with only one piece of planned wit. For years I had been waiting for a chance to use a punch-line I had heard. It required a certain kind of anonymous phone call. The odds were enormously against it ever happening to me, but for some reason it stuck in my mind. One day the phone rang and I answered.

"Is this Mister So-and-So?" the caller asked.

"No, it isn't." I replied.

"Are you sure?" Here it was! The opportunity I'd been waiting for, all these years. But I didn't leap. I savored it.

"No, I said this isn't Mister So-and-So."

The caller was getting indignant. "Are you sure?" The moment had arrived.

"Have I ever lied to you?" It was exactly as I recalled being told about it. The caller held on for the longest moment. Then

112

without another word, hung up.

I had a dean in college who was both an administrator and teacher of English. One day our seminar traded rooms with an Economics class. Ten or fifteen minutes into class, the door burst open and a large, flushed woman stood there, looking us over.

"Is this class in Labor?" she gasped.

The teacher's bland reply was, "Lord, I hope not."

I wonder if wit isn't something that comes to all of us after years of dealing with many of the same materials, happenings, and failed opportunities. As for the planned retort, many famously funny playwrights work long and hard for the one-liners they are known for. I've heard tell that Neil Simon, the most successful modern American playwright, works in an office eight hours a day crafting his famous one-liners. I prefer to think that Noel Coward was being spontaneous that day on the elevator in Sidney when an Aussie recognized him and began making a nuisance of himself.

"Oh, everybody, look 'oo's 'ere. It's No-well Cow-ward. Sigh somethin' funny, No-well Cow-ward." Legend has it that Coward looked casually at the man and said, "Kangaroo."

TEACHER AS IRONIST

I have had a number of teachers who were consummate ironists, pretending to have attitudes and feelings which were not their own. For example, one of the friendliest and least aggressive forms of irony is pretending ignorance in front of a class made up of students who are convinced that they have the corner on stupidity. The miscalculation on the board, the outrageous statement, the pathetic mispronounciation, the wide-eyed mistake about the examination date are thrown out like bread on the water, hoping for a bite. By far the most brilliant example of this art form I ever experienced was in an undergraduate class called Greek Classics in Translation. Many of our professor's lectures had to do with plays on our reading list, but one day he gave a lengthy summary of a play not included in our list.

There was an assignment for the first exam in our syllabus to read a play not included but written by one of the authors studied. The mid-semester examination came and went and then one day the professor entered the room with our papers. He was full of quiet pleasure. We settled down and he began to talk. He told us about the gradual eclipse of the study of Classics on such campuses as ours. The major reason was the decision by highschools to end the teaching of Latin and Greek. But today, he confided to us, he felt a surge of hope. The trend might well have ended. He had with him a most unusual set of exams. A great stillness was growing in the room.

"This play," and he named the one he'd described in class, "has never been properly translated and certainly none of the attempts have been acquired by our library." Time crawled. That was a recognition scene to match all recognition scenes, and its author now quietly and pleasantly began handing out the exams.

You should read Gilbert Highet's description of Kittredge, the famous Shakespearean scholar, in his *The Immortal Profession* to see an example of irony as a prevailing attitude to be used in the classroom. We noted earlier that this master teacher was able to maintain a seemingly aloof and mildly aggressive manner and not have it misunderstood by his students. They knew exactly what he was really saying: that they must do the work, stay on their toes, and not expect easy success. Highet, however, points out that it was difficult to tell stories about Kittredge. If you hadn't been there, you couldn't understand the context. There is the story, though, of that one revealing moment which spelled it out for stranger and student alike. Kittredge was gesturing as he lectured and became so involved with the point he was making that he fell from his podium. There was a moment of shocked silence, and then the professor resumed his position. He looked out at the class and dismissed the matter with the comment that this was the first time he had sunk to the level of his students.

Sometimes the trickster (the teacher) is tricked, or the biter bitten. I remember a student in an advanced acting class who was so full of sweetness and consideration for her fellow students that I despaired of ever getting her to critique other people's scenes in a meaningful way. One day I decided that she deserved sarcasm as she started her customary flow of sugar about a scene we had just seen.

"I thought she was just wonderful," she began.

Pretending great impatience, I interrupted and told her she was always saying something or someone was wonderful. Was that her taste or was she running for office? Her eyelids fluttered ever so slightly and then she picked up where I had interrupted. "But . . ." and without missing a beat she listed all of the problems of the scene with surgical precision.

GALILEO AND MR. CHIPS

It is very difficult to describe what happens in the classroom of a master teacher without actually sitting through a semester. My anecdotes are meant to help, and perhaps two excerpts from a famous play and novel will give us two more useful examples of teachers using sub-text. First, a scene from *Galileo* by Bertolt Brecht, one of the great didactic playwrights of our times. In the play, the chief character is described as a master teacher, a man of great appetites, and a man of admittedly monumental weaknesse. A favorite scene of mine is the one in which he and the Little Monk argue about science and faith.

The Little Monk puts his argument to the master in terms of his parents, simple farmers of the Campagna. The man points out that Galileo's scientific studies could take away the little that his parents and people like them have: their belief in God and the accepted order of things. Galileo is portrayed as being shrewdly aware of the man's dilemma. He has noted the Little Monk's eyes darting about the room, looking at the scientific equipment, resting furtively on the open pages of the journals and books. This man is destined to become one of Galileo's most prized assistants, but first this issue must be resolved. Imagine Charles Laughton or Anthony Quayle in the following scene. Both played the role brilliantly in their careers. The conversation has already begun.

GALILEO: (Embarrassed) "Hmmm, well at least you have found out that it is not a question of the satellites of Jupiter, but of the peasants of the Campagna!"

(Note the stage direction, "embarrassed." Also, the exclamation mark at the statement's end. The actor is being told to be emphatic but not overbearing. He is taking the Little Monk seriously but has strong feelings about the issue.)

GALILEO: "And don't try to break me down by the halo of beauty that radiates from old age. How does a pearl develop in an

Charles Laughton as Galileo

oyster?"

(This is put brusquely and overstated for effect. He is beginning to create a distance between himself and the argument he is making. It is not "honesty" and special pleading, but he is not exactly playful either.)

GALILEO: "The oyster exudes slime to cover the grain of sand and the slime eventually hardens into pearl."

(The point of the example is clear. Imagine how you would emphasize the word "slime" if you were playing the role. He is saying that the Little Monk's parents are the pearl, people who are capable of turning their hard labor and poverty into something precious. It is a supremely tactful way of putting the matter.)

GALILEO: "The oyster nearly dies in the process."

(His voice is brusquer. The man is asked to draw the obvious conclusion, but balks.)

GALILEO: "To hell with the pearl, give me the healthy oyster."

(The point is made. The Little Monk's emotional argument has been answered. It's time now for reason, for honesty, no more pedagogical tricks.)

GALILEO: "And virtues are not exclusive to misery. If your parents were prosperous and happy, they might develop the virtues of happiness and prosperity.

(This is wonderfully Socratic. We can imagine he said this with relish, enjoying making the point so well. Scoring, if you will. Now, however, he retreats, as though he suddenly remembers the other man's feelings.)

GALILEO: "Today the virtues of exhaustion are caused by the exhausted land. For that my new water pumps could work more wonders than their ridiculous super-human efforts."

(It is ironic and allowable because of his show of concern for their condition, as at the outset of the argument. Both the mention of the pumps and his feeling for his parents have won the Little Monk over. Now Galileo pretends to be a high churchman, the sort of man he believes to be the true cause of the evil which has resulted in the poverty and pain of the Little Monk's parents.)

GALILEO: "Be fruitful and multiply: for war will cut down the population, and our fields are barren!"[1]

The scene continues, but the argument is over and the lesson has been brought home by a master teacher. Note the number of devices used, the shifts, the use of honesty, as well as a pause at a crucial moment, and the apparent indications of where the actor playing Galileo should reinforce their comments with physicalization. This passage always makes me aware of the way in which sub-text allows the speaker to create tension and conflict. Humor and exaggeration are acceptable ways to express serious ideas. They can certainly be used in the teacher/student relationship. The Little Monk doesn't feel as foolish and vulnerable as he might under the pressure of his famous mentor's argument. There is a great difference between hearing "You're wrong," and a comical exaggeration like, "In the great world's arena there has never been so erroneous a statement as that. It is the mother of wrong statements." And if we can't invent our own way to make the point, then let's borrow from a Winston Churchill or Abraham Lincoln. How about a proof that begins, "As Abe Lincoln once said . . .?"

The final example is one alluded to earlier. This time it is from popular fiction, James Hilton's novella, *Goodbye, Mr. Chips*. The book is considerably more subtle and believable than the famous film which starred Robert Donat. It tells the story of a man who had failed in his first teaching position, and when he was given a second chance he was determined to do better. His first test came shortly after he had arrived at Brookfield and was supervising a study hall. "Someone dropped a desk lid. Quickly, he must take everyone by surprise; he must show that there was no nonsense about him." The perpetrator was a young man named Colley. "Very well, Colley, you have a hundred lines." The first round was his. Years later, the grandson of that boy is his student and a much older Chips is saying to him, "Colley, you are— umph—a splendid example of—umph—inherited traditions. I remember your grandfather—umph—he could never grasp the Ablative Absolute. A stupid fellow your grandfather. And your father, too—umph—I remember him—he used to sit at that far desk beside the wall—he wasn't much better either. But I do believe—my dear Colley—that you are—umph—the biggest fool of the lot!"[2] And grandfather and father laughed as they reminisced through their own children about this warm, idiosyncratic old man who had taught them all.

The sub-text is that he could be provoked and that he cared and so had transmuted both into a teaching style which made him both memorable and effective. His verbal quirks—umph—had come upon him unawares but in no way undercut his worth as a teacher. Rather, they were part of the legend.

CONCLUSION

Sub-text offers both the actor and the teacher the opportunity to broaden the manner in which they communicate to their audiences. It gives us the potential for introducing the unexpected and entertaining with the expression of a word, phrase, or gesture. For those who use it, sub-text can bring vibrancy and spontaneity to our communication with our students. Teachers should remember that it also can bring deeper meaning to what is said. Students learn to be attentive when we have let it be known that honesty and directness may be replaced at any time by an unexpected physical nuance, a pun, or the sudden creation of an entirely different person on the podium before them. The ancient Greeks signalled the possibility for this when they created several of their favorite gods in this image: wise and powerful but also ironic and full of tricks. It's a model for how all of us might want to be if we had immortality or at least time enough to prepare for our next lesson.

---

[1] Bertolt Brecht, "Galileo," trans. Charles Laughton (New York: Grove Press, Inc., 1966), p.84.

[2] James Hilton, "Good-bye, Mr. Chips" (New York: Little, Brown and Company, 1962), pp.8-10.

CHAPTER 6
TEACHER/PLAYWRIGHT

CHAPTER 6: TEACHER / PLAYWRIGHT

To this point I have been discussing the teacher as actor, and exploring the techniques of modern actors for clues on how to improve our teaching. Now we want to examine playwriting for what we can learn about shaping and planning our classroom presentations. Acting and playwriting have grown up together in the theatrical arts. I mentioned the development of a new approach to acting by Stanislavski, when he undertook the task of finding a way to train actors and audiences in how to interpret and appreciate Chekhov's plays. His effort began and ended with an analysis of the play itself: how it developed action and character, created mood, approached its audience, and developed its theme. As a teacher you should explore ways to make your lectures more interesting, memorable, and challenging. Perhaps a brief study of modern playwriting will be helpful.

Let's begin with three dramatic forms which have been developed for the purpose of instruction: the three types of classes taught in most schools. They are lecture, discussion, and reports. The first has the teacher in the front of the room speaking and demonstrating. The second has teacher and students sharing responses and information. For this type you might think of language classes in which there is a constant exchange going on between the teacher and members of the class, or laboratory sessions in which the instructor moves from bench to bench discussing the work with individuals or partners, then may interrupt everyone to address a common point or problem. The third type of class, the report, is primarily associated with undergraduate seminars and many graduate level courses in all

(Opposite) Dr. Eldon Kienholz, Professor of Animal Science, Emeritus, Colorado State University. (Photo: The C.S.U. **Collegian***)*

disciplines. The emphasis in this last is on the student as teacher, with each class member taking a turn.

By far the most difficult of the three for the teacher is the lecture. Let's compare what a teacher does in a lecture class with what an actor does in a role. The part of Macbeth may be the longest in Shakespeare, but playing Clarence Darrow or Emily Dickinson is equally challenging for an accomplished actor. In such plays, as in our lectures, the performer not only creates a character but must carry the burden of the dramatic progression. How do you hold an audience's attention when you're all alone on stage for two and a half hours, or even fifty minutes? Think of it. And some teachers do this for as much as seven hours a day, if we allow them class breaks and lunch. What can playwrights teach us about handling this challenge?

THE MODERN REALISTIC PLAY

A famous German-born theatrical director named Philip Moeller once described a three-act play in these terms: in the first act you drive the hero up a tree; in the second you throw stones at him; and in the third he comes down, on his feet or his head. The metaphor works very well. Audiences must care about the character, so the term "hero" is a necessary one. The suspense created concerns whether or not he will get out of the situation safely. However, playwrights from Sophocles to David Mamet have understood that a straight line from problem to solution is boring. What would we have if Hamlet didn't equivocate? What if Oedipus didn't push for answers and then misunderstand the ones given him? In theatre these jogs in the line of action are called complications and serve to wind the tension tighter. They are the rocks thrown at the hero in the tree. Furthermore, the audience may not only be in the dark about what will happen next but may be confused about the hero's exact intentions. As Aristotle put it in his famous discourse on tragedy, *De Poetica*, character is plot. At the climax of the play we finally know how it all comes out. He lands on his feet or head, and then there is usually a quick wrap-up when a Perry Mason tells his slow-witted assistants how he arrived at a solution. This is the *denouement*, or untying, as we call it in theatre.

One-act plays, which come closer in length to a one-hour lecture, have the same general parts but pose a more limited problem, fewer characters and incidents and fewer complications. Their structure is equally valid for teachers to examine. All plays require a problem and characters who exist in a particular time and place. After these have been given us, then we are ready to meet the central character and watch his attempts to resolve his difficulty. But early on we realize that there will be set-backs and complications. One must choose conflicts which are important and interesting to the audience. One of the greatest challenges for a modern playwright, which probably won't apply to teachers using this structure, is the need for a realistic chain of events coming out of a believable circumstance and background. Verisimilitude is very important in a realistic play. In a classroom, most of us can create a logical sequence for our lesson, but we don't need to worry about its psychological, sociological, or cultural implications. In the classroom we argue meanings, defininitions, and conclusions. The central character is ourselves and the problem is related to the subject matter. However, we can certainly make use of complications, twists, turns, and climaxes, and make our central character interesting.

How might these principles be demonstrated in the typical lecture? One strategy would be to announce the problem at the outset, then appear to find a quick, comfortable answer almost immediately. However, the audience now has its first major setback and surprise as you demolish that answer. Another solution is developed? And another? Both are destroyed. When the students have pulled out their notebooks again, which they put away ten minutes ago when it appeared you had the solution in hand, is there any suspense for them in trying to guess what the real answer will be? Never fear, particularly if it is ten minutes to the hour. They will play along because they are used to it. Who doesn't know from watching television that the drama will end just before the hour does? It's all part of an audience's willing suspension of disbelief.

In another scenario, start a class with the solution to the last lecture's problem. This would be the cliff-hanger. A variation on both of these might involve having the class provide the problems, participate in critiquing the solutions, and join in the formulation of the final exam and its answers. This is essentially the script for my acting classes, in which we are all trying to discover what good acting is, as we function as audience, critic, and performer. There is much to be said for such audience participation. During the sixties and seventies "improvizational theatre" was a growth industry in America and this spirit continues to some extent in such variety shows as *Saturday Night Live* . The audience enthusiasm which this show generates is neither tribal nor arbitrary, but comes from our enjoyment of the notion that we can make a difference.

For another example of bringing theatre into your classroom, think of doing a "Great Man" or Special Effects lecture once or twice a semester. As has been already noted, there are many scripts for you to study. Typically, a solo actor fills an evening with the details of a life with which we all have some familiarity. An historic encounter takes place before our eyes; a well-known poem is composed; a little known and highly personal side of a famous person is revealed. Because these are plays, they are meant to fill an entire evening and are designed for a general audience, but the dramatic form is highly usable in a classroom. I would suggest that you read several. I recommend David W. Rintel's *Clarence Darrow*, based on Irving Stone's *Clarence Darrow for the Defense* . This is both good theatre and valid biography. Admittedly the script has a tendency to speak of his more important cases and to generalize his life story, but there are certain aspects of this play that I find fascinating. After seeing it produced a number of times, I concluded that one of the playwright's objectives was to demonstrate Darrow's tenacity and thoroughness. This was, after all, the man whose summary for the Leopold-Loeb trial lasted three hours and dealt with the whole issue of capital punishment. The actor I watched in these performances developed a special affect for Darrow. He was both meticulous and indomitable. By play's end, I felt sympathy for anyone who had to face him in a trial. His courtroom expertise was only the tip of the iceberg. It was his research and preparation and his moral positions on a wide range of controversial and often unpopular issues which were the measure of the man. What is extraordinary about the play is its power to persuade an audience that they are seeing the essence of a man, during a brief stage impersonation. I wonder what a teacher of civics or professor of history could do with excerpts from this play, or what they should be encouraged to try themselves with another historical figure.

I was not as impressed with *Give 'Em Hell, Harry* or *Mark Twain*, though the actors, James Whitmore and Hal Holbrook, were superb. These plays work on the level of moment-to-moment

William Benton in Clarence Darrow, *Dir. by Morris Burns.*

dash and flash and don't strike me as reflecting a deeper concern for the relationship of character to the times and people. *The Belle of Amherst,* by William Luce, which is based on the life of Emily Dickinson, seems to split the difference. I was intrigued and entertained by both the theatricality and intelligence of the piece. I can imagine teachers in high school and college using scenes from this play to explain the background of some of her most famous poems. However, it would be better if you began to develop your own scripts based on an Emily Dickinson or some other figure for whom you have special feelings and understanding. Start with a twenty minute scene and let it grow as you use it semester after semester.

THE DISCUSSION

The discussion format for a class can allow the teacher every choice from improvization to a carefully plotted and crafted performance. The format is inherently dramatic, because it depends on audience participation. But be forewarned. If spontaneity and involvement are difficult to carry off on stage, just try them in a classroom. Most people, for one thing, are terrified or offended by controversy. As any television or radio interviewer would assure us, if a spirited one-on-one interview is difficult to achieve, then a group interaction is almost impossible. Watching Phil Donahue on television, we can observed one of the admitted masters of this form. He functions as a catalyst between the audience and his guests, pausing to take the spotlight himself when he feels that business is grinding to a halt. His life-line in this precarious act is his phone connection with out-of-town callers to whom he can turn when needed. And like a good director, he generates excitement. It was, therefore, an eye-opener watching Donahue trying to work his magic with a group of campaign-hardened candidates for the Democratic presidential nomination in a debate he hosted in 1984. The chosen format apparently didn't suit him or his people. The audience was too far away and his mike cord too short, and, most importantly, the candidates weren't about to be direct, relaxed, or share the microphone. It was fascinating. What is even more interesting is to speculate about a format that would work with such a group. Perhaps what comes closest is the Public Television series on public issues. In these shows a well-prepared moderator sets up hypothetical cases involving issues of law, government, and public ethics and challenges experts to find solutions. The secret to the success of this format is the intelligence of the people involved, their whole-hearted acceptance of the premise, and the skill of the moderator.

There are other remarkable success stories in managing discussion groups. Modern language instruction has been deeply influenced over the past thirty years by a new sort of teacher who interacts with students on a surprising number of levels. Have you read or heard about language instructors who immediately immerse their students in communicating in the new language? They act out skits in which everyone orders a meal or asks directions; and then students do homework assignments which require them to invent situations and demonstrations for performance in class the next day.

We are all familiar with those college courses which have two lectures a week and then break the class into small discussion groups. Experience on both sides of the table has taught me that the small group sessions are too good to leave to graduate teaching assistants. Granted, the resources of most colleges won't allow it, but they are exactly what the professor needs. In a small discussion group we can learn first-hand how our lectures are coming across and the special problems students are encountering. In lieu of this, you might try a review session for the whole class with written questions which you collect beforehand. For an extreme example of the possible dynamics of a discussion class, I recall a story I was told about a graduate seminar. The professor appeared for the first meeting and asked, after handing out the assignment sheet, if there were any questions. When there were none, he closed his briefcase and left. He reappeared the next week, collected reports, and the same thing happened. By the third week the students got the idea, and there were plenty of questions as the course got underway.

There will always be students who try to turn any discussion class into a dialogue with the teacher, and one of the challenges of this type of teaching is to structure it so that everyone participates. Be glad that you don't have the problem that teachers have in Japan or Taiwan, where students have been trained to listen attentively, take notes, and regurgitate the information on examinations. Respect for elders dictates that they not interrupt a lecture with a question, but when they encounter a teacher who wants them to interract during class, they back away. After all, a provocative question might please your teacher but could also mean many extra hours of study and memorization for the whole class.

THE STUDENT REPORT

Personally, one of my least favorite forms of instruction is the one used often in graduate seminar classes: the student report. When it is poorly done, it is an embarrassment or bore or both. It is extremely difficult for a teacher to guarantee the level of the papers presented unless a considerable amount of time is spent outside of class with each student. Unfortunately, this rarely happens. I still remember an honors seminar in my undergraduate days. One of my classmates read a particularly uninspired paper about a famous Romantic poet. It went on and on. Finally, it ended and the professor broke the ensuing silence with this comment: "Mr. ——, some people have problems distinguishing the trees from the forest, but you're having difficulty with shrubbery." I used to repeat this story, but stopped when I began running seminars. Nowadays, I'd prefer to meet with the student long before the paper is to be read, work together on its content, and then give pointers on how it might best be delivered. The reading of the paper should be positive reinforcement for the student's work, as well as a brief turn in the spotlight.

I've come to think that most seminars are poorly handled by teachers. We've subverted a good idea with our own laziness. However, I've seen them done properly. "Seminar by example" is what you could call it. Alois Nagler, a theatre historian at Yale, used to assign at least one seminar meeting a semester to each student in his graduate courses. He worked with us individually, encouraged us to use slides and bibliographical hand-outs, and most importantly, did a number of exemplary performances himself before he turned us loose. I thought he made the most of what is basically a treacherous format.

THE QUALITATIVE ASPECTS OF DRAMA

These suggestions which I have been making on how to use playwriting techniques in your classroom presentations are largely what could be called the "quantitative" aspects of dramatic form. They have to do with the structure of the event and conventional solutions for how to hold an audience's attention. Over the years I have discovered that most of my students are sophisticated about these matters. Indeed, they can guess the next plot twist in the standard movie and have no difficulty predicting the outcome of the television drama special. It's all part of our familiarity with the art and our enjoyment of it. But there is a significant difference between this kind of fare and memorable drama. One way to point to these differences is to note what might be called the "qualitative" aspects. Four of these strike me as being particularly useful for teachers who are using dramatic form as a way of improving their classroom performances.

One is the notion of a play having a "spine," a through-line which not only articulates a play's meaning but seeks to unify and explain all of its aspects. Another is the consideration of a drama's special way of speaking to its audience. For example, does it admit to their being there or does it pretend that there is a fourth wall between the performance and the audience? A third qualitative aspect is the play's mood or atmosphere. And the last is a play's underlying cultural concerns. Let's consider these in turn.

A contemporary screen writer like William Goldman (*A Bridge Too Far* and *Butch Cassidy and the Sundance Kid*) talks endlessly about the need for a script to have a spine. This can be defined as a clearly understandable meaning or theme which underpins all action, characterization, dialogue, and the design and use of the medium used to bring it to an audience. This is certainly the case with such giants in film-making as Kurasawa and Ingmar Bergman. It is also a metaphor for how creative people from the different disciplines work together on films and plays. The ideal circumstance is one in which the cooperating artists agree on the theme and mood of a production and then set about finding the best way to express themselves and complement one another's contributions. As for playwrights who show this ability, I still remember my excitement when I was doing graduate research on John Webster, the Jacobean playwright, and made a surprising discovery. I had undertaken the project of cataloguing all of Webster's metaphors in the play *The White Devil* , a great play which I was destroying with this tiresome exercise. But when I analyzed my results, an amazing fact began to emerge. I should tell you that John Webster was famous among his contemporaries for spending a great amount of time perfecting the texts of the plays he wrote alone, not in collaboration with his fellow playwrights. And here it was before me: hundreds of metaphors which not only commented on character and place, but in several crucial series functioned as preparations for action to

Zero Mostel as Pseudolus in A Funny Thing Happened on the Way to the Forum

come. The Jacobean period was marked by excess in the use of language, but not so with Webster, who exploited his audience's love of poetry to focus attention upon the "spine" of his play.

It's important for a playwright to know what a play is about when writing it; not just the storyline and biographies of the characters, but its meaning. When a play is being prepared for production, the playwright, director, and designer will agree on the drama's "spine": the through-line of action, theme, and character. Then hopefully they will go a step farther. They will search for language to express the total "meaning" of the work. Often with people from the different artistic disciplines in a production team, words fall short in expressing meaning. At this juncture they may attempt to find an IMAGE for the production concept.

In American theatre, one of the most famous examples of this process is one documented by participants in the premiere production of *A Streetcar Named Desire*: : Elia Kazan, Tennessee Williams, and Jo Mielziner. After much discussion and thought, the director, playwright, and designer agreed on the image of a moth and a naked lightbulb, as standing for the play. To some of us it may initially seem arbitrary and even silly. But think of its implications. The moth is Blanche and the lightbulb the danger of her relationship with Stanley which she seems drawn to. The visual aspects of the metaphor were expressed by Mielziner's gauzey, see-through settings and Blanche's costumes, which are both like a light seen through a moth's wings.

The second qualitative aspect of drama deals with how a playwright treats the audience. Are they acknowledged and played to or are they treated as though they aren't there? There are conventions between players and audience concerning how a play communicates. For example, theatricalism is a style of drama which puts a play right in the audience's lap. Often it is comic, physical, and farcical. The actors play "out" to the audience, asking for their attention and laughter. A wonderful example of this is Richard Lester's movie of *A Funny Thing Happened on the Way to the Forum* with Zero Mostel. The film is filled with visual jokes, actors' asides, and wild juxtapositioning of scenes. One of my favorite sequences in the movie is the singing of *Everybody Ought to Have a Maid* , during which the characters sing without interruption but the camera puts them everywhere, including the top of a Roman aquaduct.

The opposite of this is fourth-wall realism. The "fourth-wall" term was invented by an 18th century French playwright and critic named Diderot, who anticipated modern drama when he suggested a kind of theatre in which the audience would be made to feel that they were looking through a wall, unnoticed by the characters. What they are meant to imagine is that life is really being lived by the people in those rooms. This theory was later carried to extremes in naturalism. Plays using the latter convention might never use the curtain but be in progress as the audience came in, with a maid cleaning the parlor on stage and end with master heading upstairs for bed. The only familiar theatrical moment in these dramas might be at play's end, when the actors took a bow.

Connected with the question of how plays should interact with an audience is the controversy over what we have referred to earlier as the "magic gulf," that space which separates the stage from the audience. There have been many experiments, including one by the playwright John Guare, who in *Cop-Out* had an actor die in the aisle and lie there as the audience exited. And Jean Genet had a threatening character in *The Blacks* move into the audience and offer a ball of yarn to random audience members. It was never explained, and the consensus of theatre-goers was that it was interesting but alarming.

A personal experience might help to describe the feelings provoked by these "violations" of audience space. One semester I was teaching advanced directing, and the class kept bringing up the matter of the "magic gulf," wondering why it should be observed. The debate continued, so when they were preparing their one-acts for public viewing at the end of the semester, I requested the opportunity to direct one myself. They agreed. I had decided on a play by Bertolt Brecht, *The Jewish Wife* , a one-act monologue taken from *The Private Life of the Master Race*. My actress was a willing co- conspirator.

The character is on the phone with friends when the action begins, telling them that she is going to Holland for a holiday and hopes to return soon. She is packing and waiting for her surgeon husband to come home. It is soon clear to the audience that she is under enormous pressure, that several of her acquaintances are afraid to talk with her, and her husband has been acting in a way that suggests he is planning to break off their relationship. She has a last, imagined conversation with him before he arrives, in which she expresses all of her disgust for him and for the regime which he is now supporting. When he finally arrives, he has nothing to say. By his silence he confirms our impression that he has given into pressure and is anxious to be rid of her. The drama is very challenging and hard-hitting. With all this in mind, I set about arranging an experiment for my directors. I put two "plants" in the audience, and when the play ended in our small experimental theatre, the audience began to applaud and then my student plant, who was sitting in the front row, stood and called out disgustedly, "Aww, come off it!" The house grew still. Then the wife of a colleague sitting in the back row jumped to her feet. She appeared to be European, with her close-cropped hair and tailored suit. And in a heavy German accent she answered the young man: "Dat vass de vay it vass!" The audience, which had been enthusiastically applauding the moment before was stunned. They left the room quickly and silently in the manner of neighbors who have stumbled upon an ugly argument between the people next door. This wasn't theatre, they seemed to say, but one of life's awkward moments.

The third qualitative aspect of theatre which I would mention is a studied use of mood or atmosphere. Can you think of a movie you've seen recently in which the music used under the titles didn't accurately predict the type of story to be told? Its seriousness or humor, its reality or fantasy? In theatre, an analogy to this is the production's poster. Visual and auditory imagery are extremely effective because they speak directly to the emotions. Film goes one step further in that it typically uses music throughout to call up the desired emotions, and it is able to change scenes immediately, take us to the place the characters are talking about, and show us all the rooms in the home where the action is taking place. In theatre, set design, costuming, and lighting are the obvious means for creating atmospheres, but the scope is narrower and the audience's imagination is called upon to fill out the reality.

My personal taste is for something rarely seen or felt in the movies, but often in play productions: a few clues are given to the audience and we are expected to extrapolate the rest. Instead of the action being accompanied by the constant babble of background music or sound effects, a character comments on what he is hearing or the script says there is the "sound of a distant string breaking," a stage direction in Chekhov's *The Cherry Orchard* . Also, I will never forget a memorable *Three Sisters* by the same author that was being toured by John Housman's Acting Company in the 1980s. In the dancing scene, there were musicians playing but they slowly faded out as a young boy and girl knelt down on the front of the stage between the audience and the dancing couples and began to pump an old fashioned metal top until it began to sing as it spun. The dancers slowly responded to the sound and stopped and turned and listened as we all heard that strange, floating chord in the ensuing silence. A play which uses an almost empty space and yet provides my imagination with everything I need to create the larger reality in my mind intrigues me. If I didn't accept the need for variety in all art, I would always choose this style of staging.

The last of the qualitative features of drama is those underlying assumptions which operate in all art, particularly those which comment on the world around us. In theatre a genre may prevail, century after century, but the cultural understandings change. For example, we all know about Greek tragedy. Such plays as *Agamemnon, Oedipus Rex*, and *Medea* are familiar to all of us. Shakespeare's *Hamlet* and *Othello* , Arthur Miller's *Death of a Salesman* , and Williams' *Streetcar Named Desire* also fit this genre, but they are very different because they are based on different assumptions. Miller would argue that Willy Loman's life is tragic despite his status in life. Shakespeare would agree with the Greeks that great men are the fit subject for such plays, but he would have his own feelings about the operation of fate in men's lives. Even the Athenians in the time of Sophocles might truly believe that man is responsible for everything that happens to him. And so it goes.

Let me give an example of the use of underlying assumptions. As teachers creating our own classroom "dramas," we might operate from the belief that there are two great traditions which underlie public and private education in America. One comes out of the Middle Ages and the founding of universities and church and community schools during that period. One word would describe the founding teachers and their method: disputatious. The other tradition is much more modern and is linked with the development of democratic societies which attempt to reduce class differences and to absorb the new theories of child development and concepts of equality in training and opportunity for careers. There are many terms for this approach to education: child-centered, democratic, or for some of its critics, permissive. But it is one of the great achievements of American society, which led the way in universal education.

As you may know, most of the titles, curricula, and examinations for advanced degrees used by today's universities were developed in the Middle Ages. Such historic figures as Martin Luther and Abelard were pioneers in this movement. It appears that the latter's contentiousness was a quality which attracted rather than discouraged students. He left the monastery and went to Paris at the age of 37. There he attracted students from all over the world. His students became important bishops and cardinals in the church.

A lecture during this period was both an exposition of points and a defense of conclusions. Such "dialectical competence" became a requisite for all teaching in the higher faculties. The Scholastic system posed serious hurdles for the novice teacher, but at the same time created opportunities for both well-trained students and clever charlatans. Both sought out opportunities to speak and take on all comers. If they were successful, they might take on students or be invited to join a faculty. One wonders what London's Hyde Park, with its tradition of free speech and collection of crack-pots and wind-bags, would become if this system were reinstated because of a scarcity of teaching positions.

The other tradition in education is one that places the student in the center and espouses egalitarianism. There are many ways of accomplishing this goal on all levels: special classes for poorer students, shaping the curriculum to allow everyone a chance at academic success, and strategies to challenge brighter students. The fact is that these two approaches, call them the one that challenges and the one that accepts, are very different intellectually and emotionally. We should be aware that whichever we tend toward, it may color our whole approach. And this is proper.

APPLYING THESE EFFECTS TO TEACHING

Now that we've discussed these "qualitative" aspects of drama, let's consider how they might affect your classroom presentations. Probably much more deeply than the structural or quantitative effects we discussed earlier. For most audiences, the reality they experience is the one you create, to a surprising degree. The "spine" of a lecture isn't simply the theme of a lecture but a way of pointing to how one experiences it. On the deepest level it is best expressed as an image and because of this transformation will have greater adaptibility to the various concerns of your presentation. It is deeper than style and certainly more than the sum of the lecture's and the technique's parts.

Very often in our culture, when we sense this unity of purpose and effect, the word gets around quickly. Advertising lives in hope of making this connection for its products. Our national consciousness seizes on people and events that have this quality. Think of the effect of equating the Kennedy presidency with Camelot and the musical by that name, and the Civil Rights movement with Martin Luther King's "I have a dream" speech. People speak of apple pie and motherhood; and Paul Sagan tells us of "billions and billions of stars" as he stands in front of an enormous image of the heavens.

What is the equivalent in the classroom of a choice like that between theatricalism and fourth-wall realism? If you choose the first for a lecture, you might be emphasizing openness and good humor. If you choose realism, your purpose could be to emphasize the seriousness and truthfulness of the materials you are presenting. You are documenting instead of entertaining. Both of these and other conventions developed for theatre can be powerful tools in teaching.

From the beginning of this book I have been developing the notion of the teacher as a theatrical persona; but not through violent reshaping of oneself but through a realization of one's own talents and inclinations. This realization is enhanced by the use of both honesty and sub-text in one's presentations; the ability to constantly monitor one's audience; and now by the application of certain playwriting techniques. Remember that it is not necessary to receive constant reinforcement from the students that they "like" you, anymore than an actor would insist on playing "nice" roles. Their paying attention, interacting with you, and absorbing what is being taught are the true signs of your effectiveness. We all know teachers who have deliberately chosen to be gruff and demanding in class, and others who have pretended to be endlessly patient and kind while they manipulated their students into proper performance. The notion of the teacher as "provocateur" is both appealing and historic.

A last thought. What can I do about the mood of my classroom? When I do frequent workshops or spend semesters walking from unfamiliar classroom to unfamiliar classroom, I envy the elementary school teachers who spend an entire career in one room. I note my students' interest in the books, photos, and paintings I have in my office. This is perfectly natural. Unfortunately, the lecture and laboratory spaces in which I work are neutral and demand that I create the mood when I walk in. How I envy those teachers who have their own room for teaching. Teachers who can put student work up on the wall, set up tables for displays, and create a huge calendar for what's coming next. At any time the teacher and her students can look up from their work and see where they've been. The room becomes a rich record of accomplishments and a provocation to do more. I once studied in a classroom like this and cherish the memory.

There is much, much more that one could say about the connections of playwrighting to teaching, but let these examples suffice. Just remember to experiment with suspense. And always

144

to be very clear or stimulatingly evasive about what you're about. One of the keys to all this is to objectify your role and purpose, dare to try something new, and take time to script it or at least think it through. In a recent book by Philip Roth there is this snatch of dialogue.

"Look," he said, "let's pretend. You're the assistant and I'm the dentist."

"But I *am* the assistant," Wendy said.

"I know," he replied, "and I'm the dentist - but pretend anyway."

(*The Counterlife*, by Philip Roth)[1]

You know who you are and what you usually do, but pretend anyway.

---

[1]Philip Roth, "The Counterlife" (New York: Farrar Straus Giroux,1986), p.34.

CHAPTER 7
ANECDOTES

CHAPTER 7: ANECDOTES

In the last hour and a half of the workshop, after the exercises, discussions of honesty and sub-text, and exploration of playwriting as a resource for techniques in developing lectures, the moment of truth arrives for the participants. I remind them that it is now their turn to teach all of us and ask them to select five minutes from a favorite lecture. I ask them to assume that we have general knowledge of the material but are by no means advanced students. I also indicate that I would like them to use as many of the techniques discussed as possible, and then they are given five minutes to prepare.

This part of the workshop is in many ways the point of the whole day's work. It is not easy. First, there is the challenge of doing something most of them have never done before: teach a group of one's peers who are focussing on their communication skills. Some of their anxiety is alleviated by their realization that everyone has to do this exercise and they are among friends, but it is still a very difficult assignment. Our participants come from one of three populations: skillful teachers who want to improve their craft; teachers who are aware of their need for improvement; and those who have been encouraged by their colleagues or chairpersons to attend the workshop.

A number of experiences with these workshop members over the years come to mind. As I've said, this is a pressure situation. It is both stimulating and, for some, terrifying. The poor performances are somewhat predictable. There are teachers who bury themselves in their outlines, and there are others who seize a piece of chalk, turn to the board and never turn back until we call

(Opposite) **The Miracle Worker** *by William Gibson. A University Theatre Production, Colorado State University, directed by Morris Burns, 1987.*

"time." People become rooted to a spot; others pace like caged animals. However, the majority open up to the group and will try several of the techniques discussed and demonstrated during the day. I remind them before and after this exercise that this is difficult for everyone and that I want to promote the notion of their preparing for the long haul, a long career with many students, and a great many experiments with how best to communicate.

When I look back on it, there have been many memorable five-minute lectures. The vast majority have been informative and often engrossing. For example, I recall a zoologist who opted to repeat a lecture on mammals which he gives to beginning students each year. He describes the parts of a vertebrate animal. No sooner had he started his lecture this day than he broke off. "I forgot that I always have a model of a dog when I discuss this," he said. "I don't think I can go on." I encouraged him to find some substitute for the model and not to change his topic. This was, after all, the sort of thing which often happens when we teach: the lamp burns out in the projector, the students prepare the wrong assignment, or there is a surprise visitor. The teacher thought for a moment and then he climbed up on the table which was in the front of the room and began using himself as the model. "This is the ventral part of a mammal . . ." It was inspired and funny. He had intuited ideas often discussed in texts on pedagogy: personalizing and using what's available at the moment, and capitalizing on an opportunity. The humor, I suppose, grew in part from his use of his body as something abstract, something he brought along to help with the demonstration. And in this way it fits Bergson's general premise on what's funny. I remember the parts, ". . . anterior, dorsal," every time I look in a mirror.

Another excellent, unforgettable five-minute lecture was delivered by a philosopher on our campus. He was describing the Greek philosophers and the sorts of topics they routinely discussed in their writings and in their daily contacts with one another and students. It was familiar material, an introduction to Greek philosophy, but I was surprised to discover that at some point he had shifted from third-person discourse to a living dialogue between a student and Socrates. It was seamless and brilliant.

As I recall, I have never sensed with any of the participants that they disliked their field. They had had freedom of choice in what they taught, and even those who admitted that most of their energies went into research, there was a desire to pass on information about their subject. It reaffirmed an opinion I formed when I taught high school, that such educational concerns as measurement and evaluation are important, but love of one's subject is cardinal.

On at least three occasions, modern language teachers have demonstrated interactive techniques of the sort mentioned earlier. I particularly enjoyed a workshop session in which a reserved, seemingly taciturn senior professor turned into a dynamo as he helped us make a visit to the bathroom to wash and then helped us order a meal, all in German.

There were many, many more. What is so often borne out by the workshop is the variety of personal styles and the effectiveness of an endless range of approaches to teaching, as well as the universal commitment to the profession. As for the last, I like truth of a statement made by one of my professors, Israel Kapstein of Brown University. He was very complex, energetic, and opinionated but also someone who cared about students and the craft. After making the comment we quoted earlier that what we are transmitting in a classroom is ultimately values and not simply information, he said:

> Once this transmission becomes the teacher's goal he comes to know the agonies and exaltations of his vocation. He challenges himself in the classroom six to nine times a week, every time he delivers a lecture. He sweats before he begins, rejoices if he feels the current flowing back and forth between him and his students, comes out of the classroom fairly intoxicated if he has touched them alive or else overcome by self-disgust if he has failed. What he really seeks is not communication but communion. And out of such communion between the student and teacher true education flows.[1]

The statement is impassioned and it is appropriate because I can remember that that was one of the many faces he used as he taught, shifting from the ironic and humorous to the deeply-felt, He was a good teacher and shared both his love of his subject and teaching. The great ones can give us knowledge, values, and even a vocation.

I have always enjoyed collecting stories about teachers. We have already shared many of these in earlier chapters, but I would like to mention here a remarkable book which was published by the university where I spent my undergraduate years. It was a collection of essays on teachers who had made a strong impression on students in recent decades. Many were my mentors, and others were fabled characters of whom I heard. Books of this sort are a wonderful idea. Who would want a statue or plaque? Every fifty years someone from each of our nation's thousand or so undergraduate colleges should undertake such a project. All schools are living organisms and the relationship between teachers and students is the heartbeat. As an autocrat of the faculty lounge used to say in the high school where I first taught, administrators and coaches are there to keep the rooms warm and give us something to do on Saturdays. But the important business occurs in classrooms.

Variety is one key to the men described in my alma mater's book. One was a teacher-administrator, one a famous scientist whose student contacts were almost exclusively with graduate students, and he was balanced by a world-class engineer and mathematician who preferred working with freshmen. The rest were social scientists and teachers of the humanities who, like Israel Kapstein, took great pains with their teaching. They were all effective in the classroom, but easy assumptions about what constitutes good teaching don't fit them. For example, several were classic authoritarian figures. One of these, the chemist Charles Klaus, the inventor of ethyl gasoline, was so much the autocrat that his nickname, to which he answered, was King. Another, the same William Prager described earlier, never abandoned his English tailor and his no-nonsense approach. Several were superb classroom performers: Tom Crosby and Ben Brown, who both taught theatre. But so were the classicist C.A.Robinson, Taft in Economics, and Curt Ducasse in philosophy, a wry gnome of a man, who was interested in everything from the paranormal to aesthetics. It would be incorrect to attribute their success in the classroom to their status as well-known scholars, though several were. Nor could it be attributed to charismatic personalities, though several of these men were compelling and a little larger than life. Others were quiet and reserved. Nor was appearance a key. True, one or two of them were big, handsome, and direct from central casting. The one thing they all did have in common, next to their love of their fields and dedication to teaching, was a trait stressed in a eulogy written for Ben Brown by a colleague in the English Department. Professor Blistein wrote, "Were we to follow the language of Shakespeare, we might call Ben an original. He belonged to what seems to be, unfortunately, an ever-declining group of true individualists. He was, in the best sense of the word, a *character*, a legend at Brown while still alive."[2]

To give just a few examples of their respective styles, let's begin with Charles Alexander Robinson. His approach to a large group of freshmen in Classics Dl was to challenge us by pointing to a slide of the Bronze Zeus (or Poseidon) and demand that we admit that it was the best statue we had ever seen. Someone hidden in the rear of the room, on the day I heard this assertion, yelled out "No." Robinson stopped and looked in the direction of the voice. "Well," he said, "you will by the end of the semester."

Actually, Robinson's forte was the small class. As the editor of *Gentlemen Under the Elms* described it:

These small classes . . . were nearly as informal as his Monday afternoon teas. He'd be talking as he entered the room, sauntering down the center aisle toward the Olympian Heights (dais). 'What shall we talk about today, my friends? Why don't we talk about Solon? What do you know about Solon, Mr. Scott?' . . . . And with that he'd be off on a lively discussion about one of the great men in the history of the world."[3]

When I think of a Robinson, whose name is prominently

connected with archeological sites in Greece and elsewhere, I can't help but remember visiting a classroom in a small Western college. The elderly English professor whom I was observing was breaking the ice with a remedial composition class. Colleagues of this man were somewhat apologetic for having me observe him. He was close to retirement and probably resistant to change, they implied. However, I was fascinated as he slowly warmed up a group of frightened and resentful students and gradually brought off a good group discussion. It was actually brilliant and probably something he did every semester. Afterwards, when we were talking about the class I had observed, I asked him if he were a fly fisherman. He said he was and by his smile I gathered he knew what I had meant by asking.

During my graduate school days, as I have said, I was a student of Alois Nagler, a famous theatre historian who was at the Yale School of Drama for decades. The first time I met him, I was struck by his resemblance to Rex Harrison in *My Fair Lady* , but this Prof. Higgins had a Viennese accent. He had begun his career as a music critic, then had turned to theatre, became an expert on Renaissance drama, and then travelled to America and New Haven, where he spent a distinguished career pounding theatre history into the hard heads of novice actors, directors, and designers. In the required year-long survey class, he was a highly organized lecturer who used slides brilliantly. He never let them interrupt his lectures but brought them up at the end of the class to remind us of what we had covered that day. As I have said earlier, I found him most effective in small seminar classes. He was also a master of the dry retort and the balanced look. You were always aware of his entry into a room, though he pretended not to dominate. A story might suffice to suggest the legend and the man.

In the late sixties a well-known radical theatre group came to Yale to perform. One evening they were doing a play loosely based on Dionysian celebrations. The production was well under way when Dr. Nagler entered the theatre and stood at the railing at the rear of the theatre's first level. According to a spectator, almost all of the theatre students were immediately aware of his presence. A particularly vehement young actor, dressed only in a loincloth, also noticed him and moved in. He began to focus his considerable hairy, sweaty energies on this calm figure standing at the railing. "I wanna be free!" he rasped. "I WANNA BE FREE!" he screamed, leaning into Nagler. Then once more, intensely, "I wanna be free." This was followed by one of those surprising silences that sometimes occur in noisy places. The entire audience hushed and Nagler's voice came through loud and clear, "You haff my permission."

A last story which was told to me by a graduate student for whom Dr. Nagler had a special fondest. He'd just seen Herr Professor about his next project and had been handed a bibliography. "He told me to read this list of books and then come back, but when I skimmed the list, half of them were in Italian. 'But, Professopr Nagler,' I told him, 'I don't read Italian.' 'Oh, that's all right,' he said. 'It's a gentleman's language. You can pick it up in a weekend.'"

In terms of the workshop, the majority of teacher stories we share, have to do with sub-text and humor.   I was told one by a friend who was enrolled in a large state university with a brand-new instructor. It was still early in the semester, but the teacher had shown himself to be full of self-confidence and surprises. On the particular day in question, he was enjoying their reactions as he returned a snap quiz which he had given the class before. The grades were terrible. Easily the most shocked was a young woman who always did well and was never unprepared if given fair warning. She was stunned by her grade. The young instructor looked out at his class after distributing the tests and asked, "Well, how do you like my little quizzy?" A lot of students had a thought in mind but didn't speak it. However, the young woman had forgotten everything but the wretched exam on her desk and bemusedly answered his question. "If this is what your quizzies are like, I wonder what your testees are like?" When her classmates erupted around her, she blushed scarlet.

Remember that wit must have the appearance of spontaneity and be stated casually. True wit cannot appear to be planned. It can't look like a file card taken from a comic's gag box. Most of us think of the right answer when we have arrived home after the party, but there is hope. Wit may arise spontaneously from long association with a subject and a relaxed attitude. Sometimes it is planned and then you have to be an actor and give it the appearance of spontaneity. Remember Neil Simon's great line from *The Odd Couple ?* When looking at the food left after the poker party, a character says, "It's either very old meat or very young cheese." But the line itself came from the pen of one of the hardest working and least spontaneous playwrights in the history of drama.

There was a legendary professor of English at the University of Oregon, E.C.A. Lesch, who was another of those larger-than-life sorts that every campus knows and celebrates. I remember him from a year I spent on the campus as a graduate student. He was an imposing figure, tall, wrapped in Harris tweeds, shod with brogans, and there was a glint of shiny metal in his thinning gray hair. The rumor was that this was a plate that surgeons had placed there after he was wounded in World War I. I recall one incident I experienced and a classic Lesch story I heard from another student. My story concerned a class I had with him in English poets. We were studying Tennyson that week, a poet who had strange ups and downs. One of his downs was *Flower in a Crannied Wall* , which strikes me as an example of that poet's sentimentality. It's brief but it's awful. The classroom window was open, ivy was creeping over the sill, and Lesch launched himself to the window and grasped an ivy leaf. With furrowed brow and hoarse, impassioned voice, he recited the poem. Tennyson and his tiny flower never had a chance.

On another occasion, a friend told me, Lesch had started a class reading from the Old Testament. He gave neither preamble nor explanation but simply started declaiming. It seems that there were three sorority girls in the class who had adopted the habit of having a final cup of coffee each morning in their house before walking into Lesch's class. They were quite prompt in their tardiness. Lesch was mid-verse when the girls walked in at their usual time. At that moment he read from Holy Writ, "and in came the three whores of Babylon."

When I tell stories like this to other teachers, they usually share their own. Just the other day a professor of philosophy on this campus told about his days in seminary which preceded his decision to teach instead of preach. Two professors came to his mind. One was a Scot who stood ramrod stiff behind his lectern in class and read his notes word-for-word through the bottom half of his bifocals. And the other was a dapper, dynamic little man who taught Old Testament and was full of drama and surprises. Once the class entered to find him coiled on the table at the front of the room in a fetal position, ready to lecture on Genesis. Another time he was standing in the window looking like a suicide about to leap, and a third time he was sitting at his desk pounding rhythmically on the table top when the class entered and then began to talk about the Assyrians and their mounted hordes. As my friend said, from those days on he had been fonder of the Old Testament.

Stories and recollections. Most of mine have been collected during and after my college days. Before that I was not very observant. As I look back on high school, I have general impressions of favorite teachers but not much detail. A son who has just finished his freshman year of college was asked to describe favorite teachers he had in school. As I heard him a general impression of my own experiences

Abraham Lincoln (Eldon Kienholz) in class.

began to return. Actually, he and a friend had gone a step farther and had taken a video camera to a special meeting they had with two of their favorite teachers before they left for college.

One is a math teacher, Don Birch. In the semester my son was taking a course with him, Birch had started speaking of multiple choice tests as "multiplo stabbo in the darko tests." The class grew used to it. One day he announced that there would be a test on that coming Friday. A student asked, "Is the test going to be multiplo stabbo in the darko?" Birch was slightly taken aback, perhaps not realizing that his nomenclature had already passed into their vocabulary, but he recovered quickly and replied,"Yesso, for you-oh."

On trying to emphasize how simple it was to add matrices, he said, "You could come stumbling off a train downtown and still be able to add matrices." He had two standard lines used to stop students from talking with one another at inappropriate times: "Discuss it over a burger" and "Take it out on the golf course." If Birch caught a student nodding off he might say, as he did once, "Do you want me to go down to the Nurse's station and get you a blankee?"

Some of these retorts might sound aggressive, but the man himself is slight and pleasant. One day a muscular student was regaling his classmates with a description of seeing their teacher in the school's weight room. He told his friends that he was happy because he "wasn't weak like the teacher is." Birch heard this and responded, "Well, every time I walk into this class I'm glad because I'm not stupid like he is."

One day, after the students had "bombed" an examination, he entered the classroom, tests in hand. Well, here are the tests." His voice was solemn and his face expressionless. "Well, it would be nice if you guys . . . (pause) . . . knew things." And a final story. One day he held his class in a social studies classroom which had pictures of American presidents marching across the top of the blackboard at which he was working. While drawing a graph, he ran out of room but suggested to the class that the line would "come up across Nixon and continue through Jack." There were several students who looked back at him with puzzlement. He saw this. "Jack. That was his nickname. You guys don't know that. " And then, pleasantly, "All you know about in life is,""Mommy, can I have some money to go out tonight?"

Another favorite teacher of my son and his friends is a woman who has taught high school English for years. She is an attractive older woman, with a comfortable air of reserve who surprises new students with comments like the one she made when the class was almost due to hand in their semester's research paper. For weeks she had been offering to help them with their work on this project. With the deadline approaching, she had seen only a handfull. She noted this and said, "If you don't come to see me by Friday, you will be up the proverbial creek, and I provide no paddles." She also told the students one day that they were being trivial and inexact in the way they labelled one of the world's greatest works. "Don't call the *Odyssey* a novel," she said. "I have a thing about that."

The last of my son's teacher stories concerns his chemistry instructor, a man who spends a great deal of care and time setting up and adjusting experiments for his class. One day the class watched, fascinated, as he adapted the tubes and clamps for the rack which would hold the apparatus he was using. He was intense and silent and the class grew hushed as the structure took shape. Softly, he began to humm and then sing. It was Kenny Roger's song. "You've got to know when to hold them, know when to fold them . . ."

OTHER KINDS OF TEACHERS

I have an old friend who some years ago left the world of business and entered the ministry. My family and I visited him just after he had been assigned his first church. Our wives and children were at his house while we sat in a coffee shop across the street from the garage where I had taken my car after it self-destructed on the way into town. Half kiddingly and half seriously, I asked him if he'd found peace. He had been a high-pressure, successful salesman. He thought for several moments, then answered, "of course not." Nowadays he was even more convinced that life was a dangerous proposition, especially when everything seemed great and the sky was blue and the future secure. No, life was safe only when you felt rushed, slightly dyspeptic, and were more than a little concerned about the quality of the job you were doing. The way he put it was, "You're in trouble when you're fat and happy. You're better off when your eyes won't blink and there's a thin line of dribble coming down your chin."

When I last saw him, he was about to retire from his final church and start serving as an interim minister. He is excellent at dealing with difficult situations and was looking forward to this new challenge. As usual we got around to talking about the stress of his work and mine. Nowadays, he told me, he had a new way to check on his sense of balance. It seemed that all he had to do with his current congregation when he sensed that things were going well, perhaps too well, was look out at the audience mid-sermon, and catch the eyes of a particular parishioner. This elderly woman had an unblemished record in his relationship with her. She had never given him a kind word and, whenever he looked her way during a sermon, she would stick her tongue out at him.

LAST STORIES

In this discussion we have suggested time and again that learning to teach is an ongoing, non-perfectible activity which is terminal for most of us. We die trying. It seems to me to be like the universe described by Einstein and Bertrand Russell: dots on an expanding balloon which we need to constantly relocate. I wonder if all the teachers who have written textbooks aren't whistling in the dark. I know this is my feeling. This and our endless lesson plans and files of tests and syllabi can be seen as the futile expression of our desire to get it right for once and all. Of course it won't happen. Not for the good teacher. This is a positive thing, and something I've learned from actors. It has been mentioned that Olivier spent years doing Othello only to mourn that he didn't know what he'd done and certainly couldn't repeat it. I have a more modest example which happens each year.

For a number of years we have done summer theatre on our campus. Every fall we bring these plays back as "reheats" for the students, faculty, and community people who weren't able to see them in July. One of the facts about learning a role is that the lines and stage movements are only the first level of the process. Both actors and director are involved in a continuing and changing process when they address the problems of making it communicate better to an audience. One of the signposts of success in this activity is that the actors begin, as we say, to "grow" into their parts. There is greater economy and subtlety in the effects of the play. As an actor comes to know a character, there are fewer and fewer stated objectives and they become simpler and more direct. There comes a time when more background information, more thought and reading, study of the play's environment and period become redundant because the actor is beginning to live the character's life through the clues given. The very space in which the play is being performed will become a sort of neighborhood and family photo album which reinforce both rehearsals and performances. In other words, in a microcosm of our own creation we move through phases of development as we do in our personal lives. During the run of the show, the experience of the pressure cooker of audience reaction leads, hopefully, to an even deeper understanding of the play and its parts. There will be talks with fellow actors, the director, audience members, and special rehearsals called to adapt to new insights.

By the time the summer run is ended, you might think the process would be finished. Not so. One summer a fine young actress and actor played the roles of Fonsia Dorsey and Weller Martin in a production of *Gin Game*. It was a good production, and one of its features was the domination of the action by the male character. It was so obvious that I assumed it was the way the script worked. But when the play was brought back for reheats one month later, a most amazing thing had happened. The difference moment to moment was hard to detect, but now the play was an equal struggle between the two characters, and the ending was now twice as touching because of our interest in both characters. In this new version both Fonsia and Weller were losing the possibility of richness and meaning in the last years of their lives by breaking off this often brittle and challenging relationship. I asked other people if this had been their reaction as well. It was. Finally, I asked the young actress what had been the difference for her in the reheats. She answered very honestly. "I guess she grew up."

The stories we have been telling in this chapter may give the wrong impression. Teaching is long-term not short. The effect of good teachers on their students is created over time, not through one or two memorable moments. I recall a professor I had as a freshman who taught the English Literature survey course. He was slight and small and spoke with a lisp. The course did not begin auspiciously. To this day I remember his initial comment. "Beowulf," he said, "was a *wery wirile* man." One might think that after this beginning the teacher would struggle the rest of the year to hold our attention and gain our respect. Actually he achieved this in both the short run and the long. He had other qualities in abundance: control of his material, a genuine interest in his students, and abiding good nature, which ran contrary to any stereotype of people with his mild disability. In fact, the lisp might even have been a strength because it immediately established a sort of equality between us, the unknowing new kids, and the knowledgeable professor.

Teaching is long-term. There are similarities of what it is like for many of us to what might be called "layering" in acting. There are many characters in drama who demand the slow approach. I have already mentioned Mother Courage in Brecht's famous play.

She is angular and seemingly insensitive, but if the actress playing her will just prevail, a wonderful thing will happen late in the play. The audience begins to understand that her abruptness with her children comes from her instinct to protect them. Her way of making a living, taking boots and equipment from the dead soldiers and selling them to living, may not be a vocation of choice but it is her way of keeping her family together in terrible times. Her habit of distancing herself from the softer human feelings is protective as well, and truly analogous to the behavior of a fierce animal protecting her young. Late in the play, when she leaves the Cook because he will not accept her and her mute daughter, Kattrin, the audience finally has the whole picture and she begins to take on almost heroic proportions. But it is achieved through the integrity of the playwright and his character. One wonders how the typical movie company would handle this sort of heroine. We will never know, I suspect, because they won't touch it.

Another character comes to mind, from a play we have mentioned earlier, William Gibson's *The Miracle Worker*. The play's central character is not Helen Keller, but Anne Sullivan, her teacher. In many ways she is a damaged woman, who has lived through the hell of a state institution when still a child. She tried to shelter her young brother from the horror around them but finally lost him. When she enters the world as an adult, she seeks out the impossible cases such as Helen's, perhaps as guilt payment to the brother she feels she failed. She is strange in appearance and has few social graces. Oddly enough, she succeeds in persuading Helen's father that she should be allowed to continue her work with his child. It could be because this traditional man doesn't see her as a woman. Indeed, she is a passionate interloper who is first

The Miracle Worker, *University Theatre, Colorado State University, 1987. Dir. by Morris Burns.*

166

and foremost a teacher. Obsessive and cantankerous, she is beyond the bounds of conventional society. It's a fascinating portrayal and one which every teacher should study, because first, last and always she is a master teacher.

I hope that none of us will ever stop thinking and reading about our profession and ways to challenge ourselves and our students in the classroom. It is a stage, if you will, in which we play out endless scenarios and experiment with countless strategies and tactics to achieve what all of us agree are valuable ends. As Stanislavski might put it, we have our super-objectives, we face obstacles in our relationships, and must invent strategies and tactics to achieve our goals.

---

[1] Jay Barry, "Gentlemen Under the Elms" (Providence, Rhode Island: Brown University), p.108.

[2] Barry, p.43.

[3] Barry, p.69.

CHAPTER 8
FINAL THOUGHTS

LA LEÇON D'HISTOIRE.

CHAPTER 8 :
FINAL THOUGHTS

We mentioned Bobby Burns once before. He was part of my life through all the years of high school teaching. I once had a student in class who approached me when she knew we were about to start studying Burns. Her grandfather, she told me, was not only a Scot who could read his country's poetry as it was meant to be read, but was also a devotee of the bard. I said we would be delighted to have him come visit the class, and a day or two later he arrived. He was a small man in his late seventies with a thatch of white hair and a strong Scottish accent. The class was entranced and after introductions I asked him to read some of his favorite poems by Burns. He launched into *To A Louse* from memory. It was wonderful and we all applauded when he finished. I then asked him to do another poem for us, and I attempted to match his accent in giving the name of one I would like to hear. In his introduction of the first poem he had said "loose" for louse, so I took a chance and asked if he knew *To A Mouse,* "moose," as I pronounced it.

"What do ye mean?" he asked.

I scrambled. "You know? You said loose for louse and so I said moose for —"

"Oh," he interrupted, "ye mean a wee rat." And then he recited the poem.

I have special fondness for the first poem he recited. *To A Louse* tells of the poet going to an upperclass church and sitting down behind a parishioner. This fine lady is wearing her Sunday best, the chief feature of which is a fashionable hat. As he stares at

(Opposite) "The History Lesson," *(Plate #17) lithograph,* Teachers and Students *by Honore Victorin Daumier.*

the back of her head, he sees the unimaginable. There is a louse crawling on her hat. In the poem he comments ironically that the louse should realize that it's improper for him to be there. He should be crawling on a poor person, not on "sae fine a lady!" The poem ends with the famous lines: "O wad some Power the giftie gie us/ To see oursels as ithers see us!"

In this final chapter, a chapter in which we reiterate and reinforce the points we wish to make with our book, this is my first and foremost one. As teachers or actors we must always strive for control over the impression we are making. We can never know it fully, because it is a composite of reactions in any audience or class and because we are constantly changing, as well. But obviously we must learn to be critical of our performance. However, the strongest point would seem to me to be that since this is the case, the preparations we make beforehand are even more crucial than the adjustments we make during presentations. This is the equivalent of the actor's rehearsals and learning the craft. And this would truly be the "pow'r" which could, to large extent, "the giftie gie us."

Now let us proceed to other final thoughts. In the first day of my Acting I class, I make it very clear to my students that I am interested in their becoming craftsmen as well as actors. The point that I am trying to get across to them is that craftsmen know the steps they must take in order to achieve desired results. They know the standard way of doing things; ways that have developed down through the centuries. A goal I have had in putting this book together is to share with you those acting techniques which my colleagues and I have found extremely helpful in teaching. As young actors soon realize, it takes a good deal of time to master these. They must have patience as they first learn through trial and error and then discover and incorporate those techniques which work best for them.

There are two points which I stress at the beginning of our workshop. First of all, you are who you are. You have spent years developing yourselves as individuals and as teachers. It has not been my intention to suggest that you develop a "new" you. Rather I have hoped to be able to introduce you to new insights which might enhance what you are already doing. The second point is that I don't expect everyone in a workshop to immediately go out and incorporate into their teaching all that the workshop presents for consideration. All I ask my participants to do is to try some of the techniques in the interest of experimentation or in the interest of improving and sharpening their already developed teaching skills. My experience with teachers in the

I have lived a variegated life during the course of which I have been forced more than once to change my most fundamental ideas.

-Stanislavski

(The Stanislavski Technique: Russia, p.l)

In teaching the greatest sin is to be boring.

-J.F. Herbart

(The New Book of Unusual Quotations, p. 239)

workshop is very much like that I have with actors in class and in rehearsals: success breeds success. Once an actor has learned to use one technique, once she finds a key to the character she is developing, this victory gives her the momentum to proceed to the next step and challenge. It is true that in the workshops, I also notice how people's willingness to take risks builds as the day goes on. It is not uncommon for a participant who starts the day by sitting behind someone else, who avoids volunteering, and gives other signs of discomfort, to gradually loosen up and start offering more and more of themselves in the last hour of the class. Risk taking is contagious.

MORE ABOUT RISK TAKING

The ability to accept risk is a key characteristic of the makeup of both the successful actor and teacher. In Chapter 3, I commented that we begin our acting classes with exercises that provide students with an emotional transition into the day's activities, and also warms up their vocal and physical instruments. These exercises often include ones which allow the young actors to use their imaginations and encourages them to take risks. For example, they may be asked to "become a character based on an animal," "become a vegetable or an inanimate object and then adapt this to a character." The aim of the exercise is to get the actors to stretch themselves far beyond their normal degree of security. I want them to explore not only who they are, but go where their imaginations lead them. In order to do these exercises, you have to be willing to take risks. They must be willing to appear foolish and make themselves vulnerable. All of us have been trained to monitor our behavior in ways that family and friends consider correct. It is anything but easy for us to drop this learned behavior and on command to freely become orangutans, seals, giraffes, and tigers. What invariably happens is that these exercises, silly as they may seem, but willingly and fully undertaken, create a bond between the performer and his audience. They both learn that it is all right to pretend and that everyone is permitted to fail, and today's failure may lead to tomorrow's success. The learning process is as important at this stage as the end performance. Everyone learns to attempt the seemingly impossible and to support one another in such moments.

VULNERABILITY

In a real sense, what the actors in these class sessions are involved in is shared vulnerability. This concept can also work for teachers using acting techniques. For those of us who feel secure in the approaches which we have been using or those who are uncertain as to how to improve what we do, the thought of attempting the ideas described in this book may seem a risky proposition. We have to be as willing to be vulnerable as the children we used to be. However, it is our contention that the very students whom we have made feel vulnerable with our questions and exams, will be surprisingly supportive of our new efforts to use sub-text, humor, honesty, or pantomime. Our vulnerability will make them open up to us.

This idea of the shared vulnerability that is possible between teacher and class leads to another acting concept. We call it ensemble playing. In the play *The Gin Game,* which we mentioned earlier, we remember a moment in our production in which Weller gave Fonsia a long look of disdain after he looked at the dreadful hand she had dealt him. She returned that look with a blank stare and then slowly broke into a triumphant smile and nodded at the hand she had dealt herself. This process of acting and reacting and validating this experience every evening of performance is the key to the very nature of ensemble playing. The two actors breathe in and breathe out together, and in a sense become one organism.

Many solo players and stand-up comics develop this sort of rapport with their audiences. Part of the pleasure we feel when we sit in such audiences is a combination of spontaneity and belonging. The idea of ensemble playing has implications for teachers in terms of team teaching, as well. As the actor needs to learn how to be selfless and set up a "moment" for a fellow player in a given situation, so we must for a fellow teacher. We have to learn one another's tempos as well as knowledge of the field. This process calls for the teacher to be both participant and observer, a phenomenon we described in Chapter 1. The ability to maintain a "split-focus" or the "objective eye" serves the teacher in such situations just as it does when we are working alone. As the audience begins to join in the spirit of the event and the teacher/performer expands on the sense of shared understanding, there is often a palpable energy created. The "ball" is thrown back and forth until it comes to a pause, a conclusion, or is broken by some sort of interruption. I am struck by how often novice actors blame the disruption on their audience: "they seem slow tonight;" "they don't have much of a sense of humor;" or "they sure are off." Seasoned performers, on the other hand, look into themselves to identify the problem: "I feel slow tonight;" "I'm not playing the comedy;" and "I sure am off."

This ability to monitor one's performance paves the way for making adjustments that maintain the vibrancy of one's contact with the audience. It is an indispensable tool for both actor and teacher. We both have double objectives: the character's and the actor's concern about the audience's awareness of what we're doing and saying. In a sense, our "objective" eye functions even outside the classroom or off the stage. It tells us that we must prepare ourselves for performances. As we said in Chapter 3, it warns us to do vocal and physical exercises immediately before performing, and for many actors it influences the kind of exercise they do "off-duty." Activities may be structured to maximize the energy which will be available for performance with a difficult lecture or troublesome class. Some of us, like actors, prefer solitude and final thoughts alone before walking into the arena.

Several years ago, John Housman's Acting Company, from the Juilliard School, performed on our campus. One of our students volunteered to work backstage during the performance. Afterwards, she reported back to class on what had gone on around her. What struck her most was an actor who some thirty minutes before curtain had brought a chair backstage. He settled down, matter of factly, and pulled out a copy of our campus newspaper. He read for twenty minutes and then left. When the show began the young woman watched for this actor and when she saw him on stage she realized that he had been reading the paper in the persona of the character he was playing: the same attitude, mannerisms, and intensity. She thought this was a wonderful way to conserve your energy and at the same time get in touch with your character before going on stage.

The professional actor has the luxury of more time and fewer demands than we teachers do, perhaps, and can perform the ritual of putting on makeup and costume before entering the stage. She can use this to help make the transition from the world of reality to that of performance.

One of the most elegant conventions for making this transition from the real world to the stage is found in Japan's ancient Noh drama. The stage itself is always the same: a cottage-like structure, a low bridge which crosses from it to the performance area, and a hanging with the picture of a pine. The performers know all the plays in the repertory and so they can concentrate on the nuances of performance. Their preparation is crucial. In the small building upstage they sit in front of mirrors, awaiting their entrances, unseen by their audience. They make the final adjustments of costume and makeup. When the moment comes to enter the stage, they step out of this room and immediately are on the bridge to the acting area. This bridge is literally a transition from the real world to that of dreams and fantasy. Most of the characters require a special shuffling step, which novices rehearse endlessly, and this is used to carry them from one world to the next, and then they become part of the play in progress.

Minimally what we need for preparations before stepping into class is a chance to run over in our minds the way we want to communicate the day's lesson to the class. The materials to be covered should be decided and prepared earlier, and as we walk across our own bridge (down the hall and through the door) our minds are on the communication of both ideas and feelings. We probably should leave early from the meeting, the lunch room, or the hallway discussion. Remember that most actors would never enter stage without first spending several minutes offstage composing themselves.

When you step into the room, your "objective eye" is wide open. You note the class' disposition. Of course you have some knowledge of your audience. Actors on our campus will tell you that their audiences on Fridays have more energy than any others. Perhaps your students are like this, and Fridays they are almost to the bursting point with the excitement they've been storing all week. Our actors say that Thursdays are sluggish. They're behaving as though they're afraid to let go. And so it goes. By the way, have you noted the behavior of some of your students as they come out of other classrooms?

What implications do such observations have for us teachers? If we can guess our class's mood before class begins, we should be in a better position to shape it and create a better learning environment. I vividly remember my first college teaching position at a small liberal arts college. There were no noon classes because that period was the designated lunch time for everybody. Anyone coming to your class after lunch was coming with a full stomach. The result was that I found I expended more energy in the first ten minutes of that class than I did in any other class of the day. Equally demanding are the 3 p.m. to 5 p.m. classes that we regularly teach. By mid-afternoon our students in acting and directing classes need exercises and the transition which they provide. I'm sure that students in other disciplines would also benefit from a regimen like this.

The most startling experience I've ever had in regard to

adjusting to the anticipated mood of a class occurred several years ago. I was teaching a beginning directing class and we were in the last third of the semester. I had sensed in the prior session that we were all bored with the class routine: the presentation of a prepared scene and then a discussion with my leading it from a seat in the front. Prior to the start of the next class, I entered the room and rearranged the furniture, placing the chairs in a circle. All of us know the theory behind this, but I had never used it after the initial weeks of a semester. The results were astonishing. The new arrangement not only altered the way we physically related to one another but served to recharge our psychological/emotional relationships. For one thing, the amount of student input, in the way of comment, increased, and they seemed to be much more open in their comments.

This experience of moving furniture based on an observation made by my objective eye reminds me of yet another dimension of acting applicable to teaching. Actors might call what I had done with the chairs a "set-up." Playwrights have performers do this all the time and when the direction isn't there, actors will do something now to effect a later consequence. In *Death of a Salesman*, Arthur Miller scripts a set-up when he gives the actor playing him the information that Willy is exhausted when he first comes on stage. Lee J. Cobb, who was Willy in the premiere production of this famous play, gave special life to this stage direction when he first entered and then special truth to his first line, "I'm tired to the death." It reminds me of the story told by the actor who played Hap in the original Broadway production. He was making the point that the play was enormously taxing for Cobb. The part of Willy Loman is a demanding one, and one night when Hewitt was waiting below stage for the final curtain calls, Cobb crossed by on his way to his position. He was drained and haggard, and the young actor couldn't resist making a joke of the situation. He caught Cobb's eye. "You been on stage yet?" Lee J. Cobb looked at him for a moment in disbelief and then, certainly for the first time that evening, laughed from the gut.

When Willy is portrayed this way on his first entrance, it is a positive piece of manipulation. He is aware that if he conveys the exhaustion physically before they hear the line, they will be better prepared to believe it.

The positive use of manipulation is another acting technique which we as teachers can use effectively. I would venture to say that most of us already do. We have a body of knowledge we want to convey and have a plan for how to bring this information to them effectively. In addition to assignments in the syllabus, we have preplanned group discussions and panels, a showing of a collection of slides which will be used to emphasize a key concept, and a half dozen video segments that we have put together for the "slump" period near the end of the semester. Each of these has been created with an eye to stimulating the students' interest at those crucial times when experience tells us that they may be overwhelmed with the material or their interest has begun to wane. This is what we mean by positive manipulation.

In a recent advanced acting class, I took the opportunity to ask the students to what extent they discuss acting outside of class. We have a "green room" in our department where our students can relax between classes and during rehearsals. It is situated so that both students and faculty walk through it all day, but I was noting that I couldn't recall overhearing conversations about acting. I was surprised when they told me that they did discuss acting, but usually at parties. And it was an important topic. My corrected impression now is that they not only learn about acting in class but also from talking with one another.

When I present the teacher as actor workshop, I often gain fresh insights on problems from participants. They offer new solutions to the usual problems of nerves, showing feelings, sustaining class interest, and personalizing our presentations. A recent example of this would be a suggestion made by a history teacher on how to personalize the experience of students who were in a large class. He typically has sections of Western Civilization which have 150 or more students. On the first day of class he asks his students to write out their name, home town, and major. They do this, hand it in, and probably forget it, but as the semester proceeds he finds opportune times to use the information he has gathered. "Mr. Clark," he might say. "You're from Troy, New York. Can you share with us the significance of your hometown's ancient namesake?" Mr. Clark and gradually everyone in class begins to realize that they are not simply numbers to this professor.

The workshops have another value for all of us. It's comforting to learn that our colleagues face many of the same challenges we do and are also struggling to find answers. In one workshop luncheon I vividly recall, a teacher made the observation that she was impressed by the length of the careers of certain stage and screen performers. She mentioned Sir Laurence Olivier, who first appeared professionally on stage at the age of 16, in 1924, did his last major stage role in 1972, and continued to do television and movie roles until his death in 1984 at the age of 82. His last major role, by the way, was that of James Tyrone in Eugene O'Neill's

Meryl Streep

Peter DeNiro in Raging Bull

Long Day's Journey into Night. He performed this arduous role during the 1971-1972 season for the National Theatre, for whom he was also artistic director. In his last years, with his energy depleted by bouts with two major illnesses, he chose to work in television and films where he could conserve his strength and project it into shorter periods of time. He found a way, in other words, to deal with the changes which came with aging and was still able to practice his art.

On several occasions when we have talked about the need to try other attitudes and even roles in class, participants have mentioned actors who they feel are good at this. One is Meryl Streep, who seems capable of portraying almost any type of character, from a comic, singing role in *Postcards from the Edge* to a tragic refugee in *Sophie's Choice*. Another is Peter DeNiro, particularly for the transformation he performed in *Raging Bull* and the uniqueness of almost every role he undertakes. And in the last year or two many people have spoken of the remarkable impersonation done by Daniel Day-Lewis in *My Left Foot*.

Daniel Day-Lewis in My Left Foot

Again the actor has spoken to us. There are many others who demonstrate versatility and staying power. Helen Hayes and Anthony Quinn also teach us to conserve energy and find roles appropriate to our stage in life. The lesson for me is that young or old, we teachers should learn to husband our health and energy and develop versatility. We have a very special gift to share. Transitional retirement programs are just one solution to this challenge, allowing us to extend and reshape our careers. But even in the beginning of our teaching,

Helen Hayes in Victoria Regina (1935)

we must learn to make ourselves as effective as possible for the long run.

A CONCLUSION OR A BEGINNING ?

When I think back on the most memorable evenings I have spent in the theatre, I am struck by some salient characteristics of acting that each of these performances contained. For one thing, in each of these nights the actors were truly present in each moment of their character's life on stage. They seemed inspired.

The parallel with teaching is there again. We also will give "memorable" performances in which we are present before our students every moment of the class. The fact that we operate from an understanding of everything we are saying and doing will give depth to our teaching. Our objective eye will help us to make those adjustments which recognize the fact that this performance is not "canned," and that we are responding to their reactions. Preparation and technique are the keys.

Years ago, when I saw Jessica Tandy and Hume Cronyn in their memorable *The Gin Game*, there was one scene which struck with particular force. Tandy, in dealing the cards to Cronyn, overshot the table and the card fell to the floor. He bent to pick it up but before rising he shot an aggressive look at her, a look that showed his disdain for the character she was playing. In speaking with Cronyn afterward, he told me that neither the card going off the table nor the look he gave his wife were rehearsed. One was accidental, the other was inspired. I understood then that he understood the character so well that he could capitalize upon a moment that would upset a lesser actor.

We have spoken at length about the preparation that teachers should invest in their work. But let's not forget spontaneity. The willingness to take risks must be there. It should come out of both our love of what we're doing as well as our trust that it will advance us toward our goal of communicating valuable knowledge.

Several years ago I saw Beverly Sills, the opera star, on Johnny Carson's *The Tonight Show* . At the time she had reduced her concertizing and had begun to devote most of her energies to directing the New York City Opera Company. But she still sang. At one point in the interview, she mentioned that she was taking a voice lesson the next day. Carson was surprised. "You mean you are still taking voice lessons at this stage of your career?" "Yes," Sills replied. "You never stop developing your instrument." That says it all for the opera singer, actor, and teacher. Serious performers never reach the end of developing themselves in their art. The process rolls on, for actors and teachers alike.

In the first chapter I noted that at no time have I thought of the workshop as a "gimmick." Twelve years of offering my ideas on the teacher as actor to hundreds of teachers in all disciplines and all stages of their careers, has convinced me that the methodology is valid. What has been particularly rewarding is seeing growth in participants even within the framework of the full day's workshop. Another benefit are the notes and comments from past participants who usually speak about the whole experience of the workshop and then mention one aspect or one technique which they consciously use day after day in their teaching. What would it be like if all of the people who've told us that they regularly stretch and vocalize before class were to get together on Wednesday morning at ten minutes to the popular class hour of nine o'clock? Personally, I think it sounds great. I also know that we all talk about teaching more than we did before and there are many more opportunities for lectures and round-tables on the art of teaching on this campus. I am delighted to be a part of that. And in the years I spent in Taipei, Taiwan, I discovered that my Chinese colleagues at my university met twice weekly to do Tai chi. I think we'll bring this up at our next workshop.

As we all know, teaching is a commitment, without end. It is one that shows respect for the past and encourages receptivity to the new. I invite you to join me in letting the art of acting enrich the skills you bring to your own art of teaching.

SUGGESTED READING LIST

I. The following list of reading should provide insights on acting which are valuable to teachers.

Boleslavsky, Richard. *Acting, The First Six Lessons.* New York: Theatre Arts Books, 1949.

> Boleslavsky, who was trained by Stanislavski, presents in dialogue form instructions to a young performer on how to use the tools all performers have at there disposal.

Branagh, Kenneth. *Beginning.* New York: W.W. Norton and Company, 1989.

> Branagh, an academy award nominated actor and director, for the work on his movie of Shakespeare's *Henry V*, gives an account of his life, pausing frequently to talk about acting.

Caine, Michael. *Acting in Film.* New York: Applause Theatre Book Publishers, 1990.

> Academy award winning actor Michael Caine gives practical insights for acting in front of a camera. His ideas can be equally valuable for the intimate environment of the classroom.

Callow, Simon. *Being An Actor.* New York: Grove Press, 1984.

> Callow, who created the role of Mozart in the original London production of *Amadeus,* gives an accounting of his career, including the training he received in acting at London's famed Drama Centre.

Chekhov, Michael. *To The Actor.* New York: Harper and Row, Publishers, 1953.

> Chekhov, another student of Stanislavaski, describes his own approach to acting, which draws heavily on the actor's imagination.

Funke, Lewis and Booth, John E. *Actors Talk About Acting.* New York: Random House, 1961.
> Interviews with fourteen actors who talk about their approaches to acting. Among those interviewed are Ann Bancroft, Morris Carnovsky, John Gielgud, Helen Hayes, and Paul Muni.

Hagen, Uta with Frankel, Haskel. *Respect for Acting.* New York: MacMillan, 1973.
> Hagen, an actress who has taught at the H/B Studio in New York City since 1947, details her internal approach to acting.

Meisner, Sanford and Longwell, Dennis. *Sanford Meisner on Acting.* New York: Random House, 1987.
> Meisner's approach to training actors is depicted in chapters showing him actually working with a class of eight women and eight men over a fifteen month period at the Neighborhood Playhouse in New York City.

Rosenbaum, Ron. "Acting: The Creative Mind of Jack Nicholson." *The New York Time Magazine,* July 13, 1986, Section 6, pp. 12-66.
> An interview with Jack Nicholson in which he gives his insights on the art of acting.

Sher, Antony. *Year of the King.* New York: Proscenium Publishers, Inc., 1986.
> Sher records the process he went through in preparing his portrayal of Richard III for the Royal Shakespeare Company. Written in diary form, the book gives vivid insights on the art of acting.

Stanislavski, Constantin. *An Actor Prepares.* Translated by Elizabeth Reynolds Hapgood. New York: Theatre Arts Books, 1936.

Stanislavski explains his approach to acting defining the use of emotion memory, the magic if, inner justification, units and objectives, and the super objective, among other concepts.

II. The following books provide valuable insights on teaching.

Barry, Jay. *Gentlemen Under the Elms.* Providence, Rhode Island: Brown University, 1982.
>Barry provides portraits of eleven teachers who taught at Brown University, providing insights into them both as individuals and teachers. The reader is exposed to a variety of teaching styles, all of which work, demonstrating the individuality of the art.

Highet, Gilbert. *The Art of Teaching.* New York: Vintage Books, 1950.
>Highet examines what teaching is and in the process refers to how several great teachers of the past taught: Socrates, Plato, Aristotle, Alexander, and Jesus.

This book may be kept

FOURTEEN DAYS

A fine will be charged for each day the book is kept overtime.

GAYLORD 142   PRINTED IN U.S.A.